SEXUALITY IN SCHOOL

SEXUALITY IN SCHOOL

The Limits of Education

JEN GILBERT

 University of Minnesota Press

Minneapolis

London

A different version of chapter 2 was published as "Risking a Relation: Sex Education and Adolescent Development," *Sex Education* 7, no. 1 (2007): 47–61. A different version of chapter 4 was published as "Thinking in Sex Education: Reading Prohibition through the Film *Desire*," *Sex Education* 13, no. 1 (2013): 30–39. Reprinted by permission of the publisher, Taylor and Francis Ltd., http://www.tandf.co.uk/journals.

Published by the University of Minnesota Press
111 Third Avenue South, Suite 290
Minneapolis, MN 55401–2520
http://www.upress.umn.edu

Library of Congress Cataloging-in-Publication Data
Gilbert, Jen.
Sexuality in school : the limits of education / Jen Gilbert.
Includes bibliographical references and index.
ISBN 978-0-8166-8637-7 (hc) — ISBN 978-0-8166-8639-1 (pb)
1. Sex instruction. 2. Gender identity—Education. 3. Sexual minorities—Education. 4. Sex differences in education. 5. Homosexuality and education. I. Title.
HQ57.3.G55 2014
372.37'2—dc 3
2014001725

Printed in the United States of America on acid-free paper

The University of Minnesota is an equal-opportunity educator and employer.

20 19 18 17 16 15 14   10 9 8 7 6 5 4 3 2 1

FOR J AND M

CONTENTS

INTRODUCTION

Queer Provocations

Beginnings

Every September I fret about what to wear on the first day of teaching. It is a perennial worry, well-honed after a life spent in schools. The entire summer leading up to my first day in high school, a perfectly composed uniform hung in my closet: gray and maroon kilt, white button-down oxford cloth shirt, navy blue tie, maroon V-neck sweater. Aside from the kilt, not much has changed. These days my first-day uniform consists of a white button-down shirt, V-neck sweater, dark jeans, and colored sneakers. In high school I understood the uniform to be a failed attempt to flatten out differences between students: all the markers of class and gender and fashion would be hidden beneath the drab monotony of sensible kilts, penny loafers, and polyester sweaters. But now, my uniform protects me: I understand that students will look at me today, for the first time, and they will have impressions and draw conclusions that I cannot control. I cannot anticipate what sense they will make of me—a middle-aged, round, masculine, white, and rather jolly professor—but I do try to give myself the best possible suit of armor, clothes that represent a certain version of myself: plain and direct, neutral, youthful, grounded.

This story is ordinary. Everyone who teaches must decide what to wear, to find clothes that perform and protect and so help shape what a teacher can look like. But for the queer teacher, these clothes, this decision, are freighted with significance. What will my clothes reveal or conceal about me? What does my white button-down shirt announce? Can I recognize myself in students' perceptions of me? Will students see some version of themselves in me? Am I wearing something that could be used against me? These questions index the vulnerability of teaching for queers. Even as I recognize that I must survive students' use of me—vicious, kind, or indifferent—I am not sure when a student's gaze means she is paying close attention or staring disdainfully. This delicate assessment registers the uncertainty of pedagogical relations, an uncertainty heightened by sexuality.

In an essay inviting teachers to risk sharing their sexual identities with students, Jonathan Silin (1999) asks, "How does our gayness function in the classroom?" (97). Against the confidence that the teacher's disclosure of her sexuality will be educative, the question registers a pause. It is as if Silin is not quite sure what will happen when gayness makes an appearance in school, either because he comes out as a gay man or because a student discloses that she or her parents are gay. Gayness, his question admits, introduces uncertainty into education. Sexuality affects how classrooms function; but like that first day in September, when my shirt and shoes and short hair meet students' interest and disdain—and my own history of growing up in schools conditions how I will decide what counts as interest or disdain—we cannot know in advance how the meanings of sexuality will come to affect experiences of teaching and learning.

Education incites sexuality; our sexuality finds a playground in school where the taunts and raucous laughter and loneliness help us know who and what we want. Sexuality animates education; teaching and learning are invested with an erotic frisson that propels and sabotages the practices of education. This is the dilemma my title, *Sexuality in School: The Limits of Education*, describes. There can be no education without the charge of sexuality; love, curiosity, and aggression fuel our engagements with knowledge. And yet education—its practices, procedures, rules, structures, and relations—can be undone by the wildness of sexuality. Sexuality will push education to its limit, and education, despite this debt, will try to limit sexuality. This is the charged emotional terrain of teaching and learning about sexuality in schools.

The research literature on sexuality education captures stories that notice how teachers and students alike are limited by an education that tries to control sexuality even as they articulate their desires through and despite those limits. Alyssa Niccolini (2013) expands on Michelle Fine's (1988; see also Fine and McClelland 2006) work on the missing discourse of desire in schools to notice how, when schools banish discussions of pleasure in the name of protecting girls, girls themselves pass soft-core romance novels back and forth in order to talk about pleasure among themselves. Jessica Fields (2008) recounts how a female sex education teacher sat cross-legged on the floor, holding a picture of the female reproductive system between her legs and in so doing inadvertently offered her own body as a model for the lesson. Cris Mayo (2007) describes how acrimonious public debate over a new multicultural curriculum that included discussion of lesbians and gay men did not just shut down conversations about sexuality but, paradoxically, had the potential to hold the closet door open. And Wanda Pillow (2004) begins her study of pregnant teens by offering a vignette in which a very pregnant young woman tries unsuccessfully to fit her body into the preformed seat and desk in her classroom. All these stories catalog the contradictions that appear at the intersection of sexuality and education. Girls take talk of sexual desire underground and develop new vernaculars of pleasure; teachers' bodies are sexualized despite and through the hygienic discourses of science; opposition to lesbian, gay, bisexual, transgender, and queer (LGBTQ) sexualities unwittingly names new possibilities for children and youth; and the pregnant teen, embodying so dramatically the failure of a certain version of sex education, works diligently to fit into the routines of classroom life. These examples chart the limits of education.

The story of education and sexuality that I tell in this book pays homage to the strange and contradictory movements of desire. I archive moments when sexuality enfranchises new modes of teaching and learning, but I also recognize when our fantasies of teaching and learning domesticate the wildness of sexuality. I inherit this project from other scholars who point to the pleasures that schools serve up despite educational practices aimed at, in part, suppressing any hint of sex.[1] Indeed, from the regulations and prohibitions that pockmark the landscape of the school and educational policy, new sexual desires and identities surface.

It is thus no accident that I am especially concerned in this book with articulating a vision of life in schools that does justice to the variegated experiences of LGBTQ students, teachers, and families. Controversies about LGBTQ issues are often the manifestation of a more general conflict around sexuality in education, and disputes about LGBTQ issues have inspired new sets of prohibitions and regulations that all teachers and students—queer and straight—must navigate. I advocate always for the full inclusion of LGBTQ people in schools, as well as our protection from discrimination and violence, but I do so with a commitment to seeing schools as caught within the contested relations between sexuality and education. Rather than cast schools as monolithic spaces—warehousing bullies and their victims, and governed by an out-of-touch administration—I read the affective life of the school as always contested, even for the tormented gay teen. Schools are filled with the hopes and aspirations of parents and students alike; the lingering effects of a history of compulsory public schooling, the stock storylines of TV sitcoms, debates over the value of certain kinds of knowledge, and the professional longing and ennui of teachers and administrators. Its emotional geography stretches from the classroom to the cafeteria, to the gym and the science lab, to the staff room and the Facebook page, and out into the parking lot and under the bleachers. In all of these places, and amid all of these social and cultural histories, teachers and students steer their ways through the daily dramas of friendships made and lost; the raced, sexed, and classed divisions that hold some people apart and bring others together; and all the other concrete and ephemeral phenomena that give the school day its shape and texture. The complexity of this portrait of the school holds as true for the preschool as for the university.

Championing the rights of LGBTQ people in schools in ways that go beyond simply protecting LGBTQ students, teachers, and families from harassment requires theories of sexuality and education that engage the messy, ambivalent, and deeply contradictory spaces and relations of the school.

Sexuality in School: The Limits of Education is a study of the educational breakdowns, conflicts, and controversies that emerge when the relationship between sexuality and education flares up to reveal underlying antagonisms between the wildness of sexuality and the purposes of schooling. Each chapter begins with a moment of conflict—efforts to censor LGBTQ-themed literature in elementary school, debates over the purposes of sexuality education, or concerns over the bullying of LGBTQ youth, for instance. These conflicts are evidence of large-scale cultural battles about sexuality, but sexuality is also a conflict for the self. As a result, these controversies are symptoms of how the most intimate of our experiences can come to shape how we see and act in the world.

When thinking through these controversies I take my cue from queer theorist Eve Sedgwick (1990), who argues, "It is only by being shameless about risking the obvious that we happen into the vicinity of the transformative" (22). To risk the obvious is to insist that we name the homophobia and transphobia that work insidiously to degrade the humanity of LGBTQ students, teachers, and families in schools. However, the risk of the obvious is also that behind, or beneath, a controversy that pits religious, conservative parents against well-meaning, tolerant teachers and LGBTQ activists, a shared set of assumptions and beliefs about sexuality that may work to undermine an expansive understanding of LGBTQ rights.[2] Being on the right side of an issue is not enough if, in standing there, we erode the possibility for new, more expansive understandings of sexuality and learning. One can be politically correct but conceptually flawed. Yet, despite the flaws in our thinking about issues, we nonetheless make commitments, however contingent and ambivalent.

For example, I have serious concerns about how the push for same-sex marriage has hijacked other important LGBTQ rights claims and tied the social recognition and protection of LGBTQ people to a stifling form of neoliberal subjectivity (cf. Duggan 2012), but I also want LGBTQ people to be able to marry. Coming down on the right side of a political issue is not enough if in doing so we lend legitimacy to a set of beliefs that, in the end, damage our self-interest. Throughout this book I try to walk this fine line, heeding always Robyn Wiegman's (2012) advice that critique must "derive its most fascinating and passionate rigor from registering the contradictions and incoherences that arise from identificatory modalities as they fail, just like we do, to arrive in any of the right places" (171–72). This ethics of failure asks us to tolerate living in the tension between the political and identificatory affiliations that constitute LGBTQ communities and our own sense of strangeness, brought on by an unruly sexuality that may send us toward certain people and places but is also restless, expansive, and, if we are lucky, wild. This wildness also must be part of how we conceptualize sexuality in schools.

Queer Provocations

We cannot take for granted that we know what we are talking about when we are talking about sexuality. Sexuality saturates educational spaces, objects, and relations. This promiscuity is sexuality's charge and its danger. When educational institutions try to cordon off sexuality in the health class or the guidance counselor's office, to fix "sex" as a knowable and discrete entity, that effort reflects a tacit acknowledgment that sexuality moves through educational objects and pedagogical relations in unpredictable ways. Across this study I make a claim for seeing the fates of sexuality and education as intertwined: there can be no thought of sexuality without invocations of schooling, upbringing, civilizing, and all the procedures we imagine are necessary to call an unsocialized sexuality into the fold of human society. Similarly, there can be no thought of education without the propulsive charge of sexuality enabling and disturbing the work of teaching and learning.

My use of both sexuality and education is somewhat impious: my tasks are to notice the range of ways each concept is used, especially in debates about LGBTQ issues; to note places of conflict and convergence between different theoretical orientations; and to place my own project amid those debates while also seeing the conflict over the meaning as itself an effect of studying sexuality and education. To study education is to be already caught in the very dynamics you wish you could notice; our educational biographies haunt our intellectual acts, and so a study of learning is always implicitly autobiographical.[3] And sexuality—linked to curiosity and what psychoanalyst Melanie Klein (1998) calls "the epistemophilic instinct"—fuels our desire to know even as it undoes that push for mastery. Sexuality drives understanding but is never commensurate with our understanding of it. It is always too much for our conceptual and affective apparatuses.

We need to articulate a theory of sexuality that is curious about its origins and can account for its unruly effects. As Talburt and Rasmussen's (2010) and Mayo's (2007) reviews of research on LGBTQ and queer issues in education reveal, educational research grapples with a tendency to collapse queer sexualities into recognizable LGBTQ identities. Talburt and Rasmussen (2010) write, "Privileged [within educational research on LGBTQ issues] has been a tacit 'strategic essentialism' in which queer educational research needs visible queer subjects to study or regulatory straight spaces to transform in order to understand itself as queer research" (4). In their call for an "after-queer" moment in educational research, Talburt and Rasmussen summon "fruitful approaches that may help queer educational research expand its arenas of analysis, linking the seemingly nonsexual and the sexual, the seemingly normal and the queer, the repeated and the emergent" (2). Theirs is a call to see sexuality as irreducible to the names we use to find and make it; this book is a response to their invitation.

LGBTQ is a fragile construction, and I make a special effort to designate moments when the acronym "LGBTQ" feels freighted by a false sense of political unity.[4] The fractures that are spackled over by the false unity of LGBTQ are multiple: racialized subjects may not find themselves inside any of the terms on offer; the lesbian, already anachronistic, may feel diminished when she becomes a letter; gender collapses into sexuality, and trans-experience is neglected; and, most important for this study, sexuality exceeds this alphabet. No matter how precise our catalog of identities, desires, and behaviors, something escapes and then returns to mark the limit of what can be known. I am interested in how sexuality can coalesce, provisionally and sometimes defensively, into those categories we use to hold it—lesbian, gay, straight, and even perhaps transgender—but then pull those categories apart, exposing the desire to get it right and find the perfect name as a mask for a deeper anxiety that sexuality has the capacity to leave us feeling shattered and unintelligible, even to ourselves.

Wiegman (2012) charts the uncertain line from sexuality to identity and writes a new axiom for the field of queer studies that is an organizing principle for this book: "It is impossible to know in advance how anyone will need to travel the distance between her desires and the world in which those desires must (try to) live" (159). From desiring women to worldly experiments in loving other women, there is no straight line—indeed, perhaps no line at all. Wiegman urges a humility; again, an ethics of failure: we are stuck in the double bind of always inhabiting and resisting the identity categories offered, and our desires do not necessarily precede or fall in line with those categories. But Wiegman's axiom can make a second turn. Just as it is impossible to know what we will make of our desires in the world, we also cannot know how the world will and will not infiltrate our desires. We do not just head out into the world to live our desires; we are inhabited by the world, and our relation to it is equally uncertain and impossible to know. The world presses itself upon us, but we do not and cannot always recognize those impressions. Put these two axiomatic twists together and what emerges is a theory of the relation between sexuality and education. Our sexuality sends us out into the world where we must live our desires, and this propulsive quality is at the center of our engagements with knowledge. But similarly, the world leaves an impression on us, marks our desires in ways both knowable and unknowable. The world is its own elusive education, felt but not known.

This relation between the self and the world continues to thrill me and to upset my theoretical bearings. I have been and continue to be deeply invested in psychoanalysis and the insistence that we read the world from the inside out; that is, our interpretations of the world must always pass through our psychic apparatus and so are marked by our intimate histories of love and loss. As Freud (1925) argues, "Perception is not a purely passive process" (238), and we are always creating the world we are surprised to discover. But, following much work in queer theory, I am also concerned with how the world presses itself upon us, takes up residence inside ourselves, and circumscribes the limits of intelligibility. The psychoanalytic question of limits—what belongs to me and what belongs to the other—feels especially urgent here. It is a relation that José Esteban Muñoz (2009) describes as "between surface and depth" (123), and, like him, in this study I try to hold open a space between the proliferating surfaces of queer theory and the depths of psychoanalysis. Both fields are themselves organized around theories of sexuality, but far from speaking with a single voice, queer theory and psychoanalysis, as disciplines, are effects of conflicts over the nature and reach of sexuality. At times I wade into these debates and tentatively take a side. But just as often, the conflicts offer important clues into the function of sexuality for teaching and learning. The conflicts raise questions about the sources, aims, and objects of sexuality, and the expansiveness of these questions is, in part, a reply to the narrow casting of sexuality as "sex" in education discourse.

To address these conflicts in a way that keeps alive the promise of their disruptive potential, I offer a series of provocations drawn from psychoanalysis and queer theory that ground this study of sexuality and education. These provocations are not comprehensive, but they do articulate my theoretical commitments—contingent as those may be. When I return at the end of the book to a similarly contingent list of pedagogical commitments that I hope could orient a welcome to LGBTQ sexualities in schools, my hope is to give these provocations life within the spaces and relations of the school. I offer them as a call to imagine a theory of sexual subjectivity tainted by queerness.

Sexuality begins at the beginning of life.

When controversies arise in schools about sexuality, sexuality is often positioned as an intruder, arriving on the scene from some other foreign place only to ruin the peaceful innocence of children and the school itself. At the threshold of adolescence, that foreignness is located inside the body of the nascent teenager whose hormones, also imagined as invaders, erupt to wreck the calm of childhood. In the trajectories assumed by these controversies, sexuality has a proper time and place, but it nonetheless always arrives too early as an uninvited guest. This understanding places sexuality outside of the subject as something one acquires in the course of development or socialization.

In psychoanalysis, however, sexuality may bear the traces of cultural norms, but it is not an effect of puberty or media socialization; it does not infect the subject from without. Instead, sexuality begins at the beginning of life: sexuality inaugurates subjectivity. As Joan Copjec (2010) explains, "Sex is not a predicate of the subject, it predicates that there is a subject" (65). The parents' sexuality, in some sense, makes the child and then also calls the child into being. Freud's theory of infantile sexuality is difficult, in part, because he argues that sexuality comes before there is a self able to "handle" sexuality. And this child, made by a sexuality that always remains enigmatic, is the paradigm of erotic life (Phillips 1998). Sexuality makes beginners of us all, which is to say that the history of our beginnings and our beginnerness haunts our sexualities.

Sexuality is a question.

Sex predicates the subject—arriving before understanding, and calling the subject into being—and so it remains both a question for the subject and a stand-in for the question of being (Copjec 2010). For Freud, the sexual researches of children are experienced as questions about origins and sexual difference. Where did I come from and what is the difference between boys and girls, are, for Freud, paradigmatic questions—the questions from which all other questions arise. Sexuality is experienced as a question, but the answers we might variously offer to ourselves and others are, more often than not, defenses against the question itself. "Answers," psychoanalyst Adam Phillips (1999) writes, "are not a cure for questions" (3). Sexuality remains a question, and this radical quality is unsettling because it points to the subject's opacity: we cannot answer the question of sexuality because a part of ourselves is foreign, and that foreignness—often understood as sexuality itself—refuses to be known. Copjec writes,

> The human being is, as a *sexuated* being, the being whose being raises questions for her. Or: it is simply the experience of sexuality that raises the question of being by rendering the subject inconspicuous, opaque to herself. . . . The conspicuousness of the subject's inconspicuousness, experienced as a question withheld from him or her, thus persists as "a piece of ignorance" and continues to pose the question of who he or she is. (2010, 67–68)

In this sense, the question of sexuality is the question of being; our sexuality, "as a piece of ignorance," ruins our wish for absolute knowledge.

But just as it undermines fantasies of omnipotence, sexuality is also the source of curiosity. And this curiosity—so central to learning—also threatens the aims of education. Adam Phillips (1998) writes,

Integral to, indeed constitutive of, the sexual behavior of children is their curiosity about sex. One could almost say that their curiosity is their sexuality. And yet it is their very curiosity about sex, Freud suggests, that creates for them a fundamental conflict with what he calls the "ideals of education." Children want to know about sexuality, but the grown-ups tell them they need to know about something else; and they need to know about something else—call it culture—to distract them from what they are really interested in. Education, Freud implies, teaches the child either to lose interest in what matters most to her or to compromise that interest. Interest has to have something added to it, called education, to make it acceptable. (21)

In this portrait of education, culture ruins curiosity or, at best, directs curiosity toward acceptable objects. This is a conflict at the heart of learning; our most pressing questions carry the traces of our infantile sexuality, but in order for them to become part of an educational project, those questions must find substitutes in socially sanctioned activities.

Sexuality needs stories.

If, for psychoanalysis, sexuality "is fundamentally but not only a question" (Copjec 2010, 71), the question interrogates the problem of origins. Like the child who asks where she comes from, sexuality poses and then disrupts the promise of origin and causality. It is both the promise of our beginnings and a force "without why"— without, that is, purpose. If sexuality begins at the beginning of life, it also demands a story of its beginnings. But the story—where did I come from?—is written backward, in the time of what Jean Laplanche (1992) calls "afterwardness." There is an untimely quality to sexuality—less cumulative than retrogressive—as the meanings of sexuality arrive too late even as they feel precocious.

This dynamic comes into view starkly in narratives of coming out. These origin stories, so central to the constitution of LGBTQ subjectivities and communities, are marked by a romance of beginnings. Across some of the literature on LGBTQ coming-out narratives, scholars lament the banality of the genre. Each story, they complain, begins with the recognition of difference—"when I was six years old I knew I wasn't like other boys"—and then proceeds in lockstep through experiences of torment to the claiming of an identity, participation in a community, and, hopefully, love, or at least sex (Probyn 1996, Sumara 1998). Critics have asked whether new forms of identity require new kinds of stories (Loutzenheiser and MacIntosh 2004). Is it possible, they ask, to tell a less teleological story of coming into one's own, where uncertainty and ambiguity persist and are not resolved into the wholeness of identity?

These critiques raise important questions. First, how might new narrative forms enfranchise new relational modes? This question is important in queer theory and throughout this book because it requires us to notice how the stories we are telling about LGBTQ identities do not simply describe the experiences of queer youth in schools but rather call youth into particular ways of being and set the terms of recognition. Queer youth then come to recognize themselves through their proximity to these stories and construct, for themselves, a narrative that is made always in relation to those norms. Second, what can the centripetal force of these stories of sexuality—the pullback toward beginnings—tell us about the nature of sexuality? That is, rather than see these stories, however conventional, as either true or false accounts, or as failures of a literary imagination, what does the urge to put sexuality into history tell us about the nature of sexuality? This question, which plumbs the relation between narrative and sexuality, asks us to notice how narratives of becoming do not just tame the wildness of sexuality but also are an effect of sexuality (Georgis 2013). Each of these questions recognizes the untimeliness of sexuality—what in queer theory is being described as anachronisms (Freeman 2010), "feeling backward" (Love 2007), or "feeling historical" (Nealon 2001). Sexuality, always precocious and always belated, requires stories that can hold this untimeliness while hinting at other possible futures and pasts.

Sexuality is made from love and hate.

Sexuality is not a synonym for pleasure, nor is it simply pleasure-seeking. Sexuality has the capacity to both tie us to the social, making us feel part of something larger than ourselves, and to become the grounds of a politics, identity, or community. But sexuality also has the capacity to unbind; shatter social ties; produce feelings of loss, disappointment, or ecstatic loneliness; and undo illusions of identity, politics, and relationality. And all these possibilities can be a source of pleasure or nonpleasure. This ambivalence—that sexuality is made from love and hate, often for the same object—is a feature of the relationship between sexuality and education.

This ambivalence causes tension both for the self who must tolerate the confusion of feelings evoked by sexuality and for the fields that study sexuality and might wish sexuality could mean one thing. In recent conversations in queer theory, this tension has emerged in what is being called the "antisocial thesis." Precipitated by the publication of Lee Edelman's (2004) polemic *No Future: Queer Theory and the Death Drive*, which insists that queerness is a refusal to participate in the promise of the future, embodied in the figure of the Child, the antisocial thesis disputes the political function of queer sexualities. The hope that queerness could hold people together in contingent political formations, create new collectivities, or inspire antinormative pedagogical dreams is contrasted with the ways that sexuality can dissolve social bonds, leading to self-shattering, alienation, and dissimulation. Can these qualities precipitate new queer subjectivities or politics? Across special issues, invited panel presentations, "feel tanks," and edited collections, scholars working in queer theory argue, rebut, propose, and push the limits of these questions. The conversation itself—a ferocious reply to rumors of the death of queer theory—would seem to suggest that the study of queerness, at least, pulls people into networks of belonging. But I also suspect that the resuscitation of queerness and the invocation across queer theory of utopias, optimism, and political fantasies work against the aggressiveness and nonutility of sexuality. But those moves, from self-shattering to social bonds and back again, trace the vicissitudes of sexuality. This study moves between understanding sexuality as excessive, asocial, and unconscious, and queerness as a strategy for and effect of living with those contradictions.

Sexuality is a human right.

These provocations—to think of sexuality as inaugurating subjectivity, as persisting as an unanswerable question in the self, as mired in love and hate, and as subject to narrative—put tremendous pressure on the concept of education. Education is entangled in the same troubles. The desire for mastery and absolute knowledge defends against the helplessness that learning introduces; our relations to knowledge are bound to be caught up in love and hate; questions, which remain an ambivalent object of education, are both exciting and hazardous; and the stories we tell about education risk holding the difficulty of learning at bay.

This portrait of sexuality and education offers lessons for a study of LGBTQ students, families, and teachers. If sexuality is a human right—as the efforts to include LGBTQ students, families, and teachers in schools propose—then these complicated relations are our humanity. The push for full recognition of the human rights of LGBTQ people and communities needs to begin with a theory of sexuality that tolerates the ambivalent and contested relation we have to the categories that name us and that we use to name ourselves. We are all entitled to what Avery Gordon (2004) calls "a complex personhood." Critiquing the tendency in social science research to equate persons with social markers—a poor person becomes defined by his or her poverty, the African American is lost behind a static conception of race, and the lesbian is understood only through her sexuality—Gordon demands that we notice, in our reading and research practices, the complicated relationship that individuals have both to the particularities of their lives and to the social categories we use to make sense of the world. In a beautiful list that attempts to repair the hubris of sociologists, Gordon writes, "Complex personhood means that all people (albeit in specific forms whose specificity is sometimes everything) remember and forget, are beset by contradiction, and recognize and misrecognize themselves and others" (4). She goes on to insist that we are all stuck and have the capacity for transformation, come together to act while also disagreeing, and are haunted by presences we both know and don't know: "At the very least, complex personhood is about conferring the respect on others that comes from presuming that life and people's lives are simultaneously straightforward and full of enormously subtle meaning" (5).

To heed Gordon's advice and recognize the straightforward as well as the subtle meanings of people's lives, our vision for the rights of LGBTQ students, teachers, and families would—like her list—make claims for the right to an ordinary life. No longer would it be enough to insist that LGBTQ people have a right to live free of harassment. Instead, those of us thinking about education would be charged with imagining and creating conditions for LGBTQ students, teachers, and families to lead full lives in schools—full of affirmation and acceptance but also of contradiction, forgetting, and misrecognition. This complexity is an effect of our sexuality; so, to welcome sexuality into the school, we must make room as well for our unintelligible selves. We can invite sexuality into the school, but we cannot know in advance who or what will arrive—and this impossibility marks the limit of an education committed to mastery.

These provocations, however partial, invested, and conflicted, name my theoretical bearings. But these bearings are restless and refuse to stay still; like Sedgwick's elaboration of a reparative reading position, the provocations are a response to loss, and the losses are multiple: the injuries that make subjectivity and the difficulties that can mar a queer life. Distinguishing between reparative modes of knowing from paranoid structures of thought, Sedgwick (2003) argues that paranoia is a strong theory that anticipates and finds confirmation of its beliefs everywhere, while in the reparative mode, the knowing subject risks surprise:

> To read from a reparative position is to surrender the knowing, anxious paranoid determination that no horror, however apparently unthinkable, shall ever come to the reader *as new;* to a reparatively positioned reader, it can seem realistic and necessary to experience surprise. Because there can be terrible surprises, however, there can also be good ones. (146)

The reparative position recognizes that "people are fragile" (Hanson 2011, 105). We are injured already, from both the terrible and good surprises, and as a condition of entering the social and securing the love of others. In the reparative position, this injury, if or when we can bear it, blurs the boundaries between inside and outside, right and wrong. We are always already compromised. This compromised self—riddled by contradictions; injured, in part, by sexuality—is at the center of pedagogical relations. Could education begin with this fragile subject? And could an antihomophobic and antitransphobic inquiry recognize the ordinary fragility of the LGBTQ subject?

Structure of the Book

This book was written in fits and starts over many years. One chapter had its beginning in my dissertation; others were drafted through births, deaths, breakups, falling in love, long semesters teaching, and over my first sabbatical. I was surprised, therefore, when I read all of the chapters start to finish and discovered, again, that I had been writing my way into a similar set of concerns over and over from slightly different vantages, through the undulating rhythm of everyday life.

These concerns, which I have outlined in this introduction, continue to feel urgent. In the chapters that follow I bring these concerns to the pedagogical relationships that constitute the everyday life of educational institutions—especially the recognitions and misrecognitions that are the danger and potential of relations between adults and children and youth. Because adults have all survived their own childhoods and adolescences, their engagements with contemporary children and youth, as well as with discourses of development, are haunted by affective histories that find symptomatic representation in the worries, anxieties, and hopes that adults have for children and youth. Discussions of sexuality and children and youth are filled with adults' own, largely unarticulated, emotional conflicts. This investment can be an act of love and care and a calling of children and youth into a world that is waiting for them, but this investment risks misrecognizing children and youth as representations of the adults' narcissism. It is a generational dynamic that I will describe as Oedipal, drawing on psychoanalytic theories of development. But psychoanalysis is not the only description of this conflict. Hannah Arendt (2006) declares, "The essence of education is natality" (171). "We are born into the world as strangers," she argues, and despite the uncertainty the strange ushers in, it is "the fact of natality" that makes possible a new beginning; "the newcomer possesses the capacity of beginning something anew" (9). This newness, however, threatens to overthrow the old, and so children and youth are received by their parents and the wider community as both a promise and a menace.

Each chapter is located in this conflict, and the portrait of intergenerational relationships that emerges respects both the promise of the new and the durability of the old. Chapter 1 begins with a juxtaposition: What is the relationship between "the queer child" and the LGBTQ adult? That is, to what use do LGBTQ adults put their childhoods? And how does the articulation of an LGBTQ identity require a history rooted in childhood experience? In my first iteration of the adult–child pedagogical relation, I argue that the invention of a childhood that could bolster our claims to a coherent LGBTQ identity neglects contemporary children whose sexualities may or may not be legibly queer. Looking at two court cases—one about the censorship of children's picture books that portray same-sex families and one about the inclusion of a trans-woman in a "women-only" rape crisis center—I explore what happens when the equality-seeking claims of LGBTQ adults rest on an inaugurating story of a queer childhood.

Chapter 2 follows the child into adolescence and considers how the idea of risk separates the conflicts of adolescence from the achievement of adulthood. I argue that adults' sense of their own "grownupness" is put under pressure by the acting out of youth. Working closely with psychoanalytic theories of adolescent development, I analyze a short story by David Leavitt that frames as an emotional problem the decision to have safer sex. The story, and the conflicts of love and loss the story describes, open up the problem of sex education to the vicissitudes of affective life.

Chapters 3 and 4 elaborate on these dynamics. Each centers on a representation of a pedagogical relationship between adults and youth. Chapter 3 examines the antibullying video project *It Gets Better*, and chapter 4 looks at a documentary film, *Desire*, which chronicles the lives of teenage girls in and around New Orleans. In *It Gets Better* and *Desire*, adults call young people into stories about the horizons of their desire. The *It Gets Better* project was started as a response to media coverage of the suicides of young gay men; it asks ordinary LGBTQ adults to share stories of a future when their sexual identity is not only a source of pain and ostracism but also a site of pleasure and love and hope. I explore how that call into a future sets the terms for what a good gay life can look like while also offering youth the narrative resources to construct stories for themselves.

In chapter 4, I focus on the ubiquity of the prohibition in sex education; everywhere youth turn they will meet some version of an adult no. Drawing on theories of thinking from psychoanalysis I make the counterintuitive claim that sometimes a prohibition can create the conditions for thinking. When Peggy, one of the subjects of the film *Desire*, meets her parents' and her schools' rules about having sex, she decides to become a sex researcher, asking her friends what they think about when they think about sex. This, I argue, is a model for a thoughtful sex education.

In chapter 5 I consider how this orientation to the problem of sexuality and education can guide the kinds of welcome we offer LGBTQ students, teachers, and families in schools. Drawing on Derrida's essay on hospitality I offer three examples in which schools are called upon to open their doors to the wildness of sexuality: debates about marriage equality and its impact on public schooling, welcoming the transitions of transgender students, and a more personal story of tolerating the irruption of sexuality in a class on adolescence. From there, I outline a reluctant manifesto for welcoming LGBTQ issues, students, teachers, parents, and community members into the spaces and relations of education. What is required to open the door of the school to whomever and whatever turns up? What kinds of stories of sexuality can find legitimacy in schools? My commitment is to understanding how schools can become places where we tolerate our perennial beginnerness, where the questions of sexuality can inspire the researches of students and teachers; where love, intimacy, and loss can become part of the affective register of sex education; and where everyone is free to explore the impossible routes between their desires and the world in which those desires must try to live.

1 BACKWARD AND FORWARD
Narrating the Queer Child

IN 1993 EVE SEDGWICK RISKED A THOUGHT that remains as provocative now as it was then: How to bring our kids up gay? This question names the pedagogical dilemma at the center of this chapter. Sedgwick did not punctuate her title with a question mark. Instead, "how to bring your kids up gay" is delivered straight-faced as a parody of parenting manuals. The mock sincerity of the title critiques the taken-for-granted status of children's heterosexuality and unmasks the barely hidden desire (or worry) that parents might be able to determine their child's sexual orientation.

The title continues ("The War on Effeminate Boys") revealing that behind the parenting manual and its omnipotent belief that parents can determine who their children will become lies a murderous impulse, the violence of which is often hidden. Sedgwick (1993) argues, "This society wants its children to know nothing; wants its queer children to conform or (and this is not a figure of speech) die; and wants not to know that it is getting what it wants" (3). This subterfuge obscures the violence of the demand for conformity, a violence that continues to haunt adult sexual subjectivities. For the queer adult, the child who survived—that is, the child that person once was—continues to exert a force on the present, insisting on her due, and so the queer adult, in an act of reconstructive imagination, calls that child into being. The queer adult, in a sense, brings up that child—her lost child—to be gay.

Sedgwick's initial argument hinges on a concurrence: the 1980 edition of the American Psychiatric Association's *Diagnostic and Statistical Manual* (DSM) was the first not to include homosexuality as a mental disorder. However, that edition, cel-ebrated for depathologizing homosexuality, also introduced a new disorder, one that allowed physicians to pathologize signs of gender nonconformity often associated with gayness. Gen-der Identity Disorder (GID), the symptoms of which are a virtual catalog of queerness in childhood, pathologizes children who too strongly identify with the opposite sex. Tomboys, sissies, or gender-independent kids could all be identified by the rubric of GID. For Sedgwick, the increasing social acceptance of gay adults is made on the backs of children who must now hew closely to gender normativity and the promise of heterosexuality, lest they grow up to become gay. In the circus of negation, "the proto-gay child," as Sedgwick names him, must live out the adult's fantasy of childhood as innocent and ignorant, and not precociously adopt a sexuality—a gay sexuality—that is properly adult. (For Sedgwick, signs of gender trouble in childhood portend a queer future.) Though homosexuality is no longer a mental disorder, the DSM refuses a path from childhood to queerness that isn't pock-marked by pathology.[1]

The temporal disorientation of these moves preoccupies me throughout this book. Gender Identity Disorder—and its recent, friendlier progenitor, Gender Dysphoria—tell the story of child-hood forward, pathologizing sissies and tomboys and ultimately offering the fragile grounds of a legitimate transgender childhood. Can childhoods anticipate certain kinds of adulthoods? And—here enters the murderous impulse Sedgwick points to—can fix-ing hints of something (some longing, some deficit, some swish) in childhood eradicate the emergence of queer adulthoods? Or, as the recent debates over transgender childhoods suggest, can protecting and even validating what is being called gender inde-pendence or creativity keep open the conditions for a possible transgender adulthood? Do transgender adults need a transgen-der childhood in order to stake a claim on their adult identity? Complicit in this anticipatory logic is the LGBTQ adult who, hav-ing survived, invents the child who could tell his or her own story forward. The childhoods of LGBTQ adults, retrospectively reconstructed in narratives of development, anchor the possibility of a coherent and stable sexual and gender identity.

Elspeth Probyn (1996) echoes Sedgwick's critique in her discussion of gay and lesbian writers' stories of childhood. Probyn notices how positioning childhood as the ontological origin of a lesbian and gay adulthood shares a logic with quantitative studies of childhood that seek to establish a causal relation between a boy's failed masculinity and his claiming a gay identity as an adult. When LGBTQ adults tell their stories backward and attempt to locate, in childhood, the source of their difference, this explanatory regime emboldens empirical researchers to try to tell the story forward and identify and quantify signs of gayness in children. In his study of narratives of transsexual embodiment, Jay Prosser (1998), as well, worries that the search for origins of a trans-identity risk becoming complicit with medicalized discourses of transsexual identity formation, propping up a new normative trajectory for the development of a transgender identity. Prosser, Probyn, and Sedgwick all ask us to notice how we deploy childhoods in the name of LGBTQ equality. One goal of this book, and this chapter then, is to be suspicious of the bad company we might be keeping in our efforts to expand rights for LGBTQ adults.

The fight for LGBTQ equality is made in these tensions—between children who are living through the present and childhoods long since lived. The injuries of childhood can be repaired through political commitments made in adulthood, and lives of contemporary children are often the scene on which we act out those commitments—with children, and their purported innocence, standing as pawns in the projective to-and-fro of political maneuvering. For the queer adult, this dynamic is fraught. Historically, LGBTQ rights have been defined as belonging to adults. The major campaigns for LGBTQ equality in North America center on rights virtually exclusive to adults: the right to privacy, access to state pensions, health care and survivor benefits, reforming age-of-consent laws, decriminalizing homosexual activity, and legislating marriage equality, for instance. Children, meanwhile, lack privacy, access most state benefits through their parents, and are not able to consent to sex or marriage. Children's anteriority to these rights and responsibilities of full citizenship makes the question of the relation between LGBTQ rights and children fraught. Indeed, rather than having a right to representations of LGBTQ life, for instance, these debates position children as in need of protection from LGBTQ issues, people, and desires. As Jessica Fields (2004) argues, "The recent successes for adults seeking the right to enter same-sex marriages or a fundamental right to private same-sex sexual expression threaten to exacerbate the already oppressive sexual conditions with which young people contend" (14). Same-sex marriage risks affirming conservative views of sexual life in sex education, and the emphasis on the right to privacy opens up public displays of LGBTQ sexuality to scrutiny—two issues that disproportionately affect children and young people since they are required to attend school and have no right to privacy when they live with parents and guardians. When LGBTQ issues come into contact with children and childhood—for example, in sex education or family life education—children's right to information is subordinate to parents' right to determine the moral and religious education their children receive.

Children's status as "not-yet" citizens is, as Cris Mayo (2006) argues, a "particular problem for liberal theory and for queer theory." She writes:

> For liberals, children are nascent citizens who must be educated in a context where liberal values and practices inculcate them into full participation as citizens. For queers, too, children are often future participants in queer communities, but queers may have no say in how those future community members are raised. (472)

The problem is twofold. Liberals assume that all children will be welcomed as citizens when they reach the age of majority, while queers cannot know in advance which children will become "future participants in queer communities." And the liberal promise of citizenship for all (that is, all who are old enough)—a central tenet of public education—is undermined by continuing state-sanctioned discrimination against queers, people of color, and poor people, among others. The rights and responsibilities of citizenship are distributed unequally in liberal democracies. And because the queer citizen is, by definition, an adult, we cannot identify future queers when they are children to offer them respite from the homophobic hatred, derision, and dismissal that are too often an ordinary part of growing up and that queer communities promise to ease. Protected neither by the state, schools, nor often by their families, children who might be "future participants in queer communities" have no rights to a queer future that may or may not arrive.

With the recent focus on marriage equality and the legitimation of LGBTQ families, LGBTQ communities have worked to crack open the claustrophobia of the nuclear family and broaden the bounds of queer community, often by having children themselves, while distancing themselves from the proto-gay child for fear of being seen as predatory and corrupting. Under the homophobic anxiety that lesbian and gay adults represent a threat to children, LGBTQ communities are at pains to demonstrate that, for instance, gay men don't, as a group, prey on young boys; that lesbian parents don't produce effeminate boys; and that gayness is not socially or genetically contagious.[2]

The intensity of these proximal relations—just how closely together can we bring adult LGBTQ sexualities and children without igniting controversy?—belies an intimacy between the queer and the child. Indeed, current debates in queer theory confirm this kinship. Kathryn Bond Stockton (2009) traces the figure of the child across representations of queer sexuality, arguing that the child embodies the delay that supposedly marks adult homosexuality and also holds open an imaginative space for affiliations and affects that will not settle down into grown-up versions of identity. The child—in surplus and deficit, precocity and delay—figures the queer who is likewise always not enough and too much, too early and too late. The untimeliness of the queer and her intimacy—conceptual and otherwise—with the child has been brought to vivid life in a range of scholarship in the theoretical humanities, but this work has yet to inform how LGBTQ issues enter conversations in the field of education.

In educational debates, we are reluctant to see children themselves as gay, lesbian, or otherwise queer, nor are there narratives in education that would celebrate the emergence of a queer identity in adolescence. Yet despite this underlying prejudice that queerness in children is not age-appropriate and is instead a developmental pathology, there is a parallel if contradictory expectation that antihomophobia education ought to begin in primary school before impoliteness becomes hardened into prejudice. The goal is to cultivate attitudes of tolerance and generosity toward the difference that is queerness and to protect the children of LGBTQ parents from abuse and bullying. These well-meaning efforts to inculcate tolerance too often fail, perhaps because the specter of the pathological queer child undermines our messages of inclusivity and respect. How can we push for the civil and human rights of LGBTQ students if we regard being or becoming gay as, at best, an unfortunate accident of genetics or environment? This hidden prejudice—that being gay is best avoided, if possible—creates an educational conundrum. We teach children to be kind to all sorts of people while secretly hoping that they won't be different at all. Insofar as education involves the bringing up of children, we bring up our children with the expectation that they will be heterosexual and will feel at home in the bodies into which they are born.

Part of the difficulty this conundrum registers lies in the conflicts within the concept of "the child"—the focus of this chapter. These children we talk about, the children who creep into these debates and who need our protection, are multiple. They include, for instance, those contemporary children who are required by law to attend school; "the child" who is subject to and the subject of political and educational discourse; the children we once were, never were, or wished we could have been; the children we do or hope to parent, and all those children excluded from the embrace of the category of "the child" because their claim on childhood has been revoked by race, poverty, or a precocious sexuality (cf. Fields 2005; Stockton 2009). Like a band of surly misfits, these political, social, historical, and psychical children move through the arguments for and against the expansion of LGBTQ rights. Try to keep track of these children, following them as they play hide-and-seek in the thicket of arguments being made for and against the extension of LGBTQ rights, especially as those rights become part of contemporary educational debate.

Beginning with a portrait of "the child" as not just multiple but conflicted in educational discourse and queer theory, "the child"—both real and recounted—is freighted with the affective histories of the adult who narrates her. This is an argument I make throughout this book, and it needs to be made more than once. "The child" is a powerful alibi for adult desires. It is as if, through education, adults construct a proxy who will carry their desires forward into the world, but in doing so, they obscure the source of those desires through appeals to "the child" and her best interests. Revealing the architecture of these plans is not only about catching the adult out—for surely the child needs the adult's desire and, at best, experiences this investment as love and care. One goal of this project is to sketch a fuller portrait of "the child" in education and in debates about LGBTQ rights, creating space inside those quotation marks so that "the child" can become more than a concept and find some breathing room as an experience, a subjectivity, or a memory.

In the rest of the chapter I make several detours. First, I trace "the child" as an effect of conflicts over its meanings; "the child" is overdetermined and so saturated with meaning but also empty and available as a screen for adult desires. Second, I follow this concept of the child through two court cases that sought to defend and extend understandings of LGBTQ rights. In the equality-seeking claims of LGBTQ adults, how is "the child" made to prop up the edifice of an adult queer identity? Third, drawing on both these discussions, I make some tentative claims for the queer child in education, a child whose relations with current debates about LGBTQ issues in schools are anything but secure. Inheriting the conflicts that Sedgwick locates in the "proto-gay child," the queer child upsets progressive narratives of LGBTQ identity development, ironically calling attention to those children whose future sexualities cannot easily be read by their gender play. One of my more difficult tasks in this volume is to insist on the importance of an antihomophobic and antitransphobic inquiry and to explore the gaps between that inquiry and the dream of education, here powerfully represented by the queer child.

Fixing "the Child"

Across these conversations and debates, "the child" serves as a repository for adults' hopes, wishes, disappointments, aggressions, and longings. In this position, "the child" bears the burden of representing not only politics and the possibility of the future, as Lee Edelman (2004) forcefully argues, but the vulnerable origins of our humanity. Because we were all once children, "the child" is our beginning. This positioning of "the child" as the origin of the adult obscures children's alterity—their sheer difference from the adults' use of them. Instead, "the child," now fixed securely within the epistemological safety of quotation marks, is an overdetermined figure, indeed a figure of overdetermination.

Psychoanalysis has a particular understanding of the process of overdetermination. An object is overdetermined when it comes to stand in for a whole series of conflicts that can and cannot be spoken. According to Laplanche and Pontalis's (1973) dictionary of psychoanalytic concepts, Freud understood overdetermination as working in two ways. First, an object is overdetermined when the "formation in question is the result of several causes, since one alone is not sufficient to account for it" (292). In this case, "the child" cannot be reduced to a single or primary cause.

It is not, in the end, either historical or biological; what comes to be known as "the child" is an effect of the relationships among social, historical, political, psychological, and biological factors. This sense of overdetermination comes close to Foucault's (1990) discussion of the "great strategic unities" of sexuality and knowledge (103). Foucault emphasizes that sexuality, in this case, is never just one thing but is an effect of a dense, contradictory set of power relations that, at times, coalesce around specific nodal points. He names four such nodal points or "strategic unities": the hysterization of women's bodies; the socialization of procreative behavior; a psychiatrization of perverse pleasure; and, most relevant here, the pedagogization of children's sex (104–5). The nominalizations (hysterization, socialization, psychiatrization, pedagogization), however unwieldy, reflect a process in the history of ideas. An activity, understood as temporary or fleeting, is turned into a noun—a thing-in-itself—that names that process; behaviors thus became fixed as identities.

Foucault's best-known formulation of this process was his description of the transformation of sodomy (the activity) into the homosexual (a type of person): "the sodomite had been a temporary aberration [someone who had a 'type of sexual relations']; the homosexual was now a species" (43). In a similar fashion, the "pedagogization of children's sex" describes how children went from displaying certain kinds of behavior, doing certain kinds of things, into being a specific kind of problem with a history, a nature, and a developmental trajectory. The problem was tied to their temporal location: "children were defined as 'preliminary' sexual beings, on this side of sex, yet within it, astride a dangerous dividing line" (104). The problem of children's precarious position at the threshold of sexuality is constructed through a range of discourses. As Foucault describes it, "Parents, families, educators, doctors, and eventually psychologists would have to take charge, in a continuous way, of this precious and perilous, dangerous and endangered sexual potential" (104). Through this process of pedagogization, children's sex became a problem for and of education, but "the child" and its nature also now came to represent sexuality itself. In this sense, "the child" is an effect of what Foucault calls "the tactical polyvalence of discourses"(100): "the child" comes into being through the cacophony of various discourses of children and childhood, but then "the child," in its singularity and fixity, obscures that history and noise. "The child," as an effect of these conflicts, marks a struggle and yet conceals its size and reach.

The second definition of overdetermination in psychoanalysis has similar properties. In this definition, "the child" is a "compromise formation." That is, as a symptom of unconscious conflict, "the child" stands as a compromise between the wish and its defense: "the child" both represents and defends against desire and its limits. Beginning with his theory of dreams, Freud understood certain phenomena—jokes, dreams, slips of the tongue, neuroses—to be attempts to represent intolerable desires as well as defend against their emergence. These "compromise formations" are overdetermined in the sense that they carry the weight of this history of internal conflict. To pick up on Foucault's formulation of "the child" on the precipice of sexuality, "the child" is a compromise formation in which the desire to know meets the opacity of sexuality. But as Britzman (2003) explains, the dreamlike qualities of "the child" are disavowed through the wish for mastery, a wish that places "the child" at the center of adult subjectivity:

> The dominant tendency [in education] is to choose the empirical child over the dream, the child the adult can know and control. But in so doing, education has reduced the child to a trope of developmental stages, cognitive needs, multiple intelligences, and behavioral objectives. And these wishes defend against a primary anxiety of adults: what if the dream of learning is other to the structures of education? (53)

"The empirical child" is the child who emerges from the pedagogization of children's sex. Defined by her capacities and deficiencies, she is emptied out and made vacant so that she can be filled up with the wishes of adults. She is a screen for the projections of adult desires, but that screen, because it exists outside of the adult, keeps those desires in play and at bay.

Reminiscent of how Sedgwick describes the disguised wishes of a homophobic society, the child allows us access to a compromised version of what we want, without knowing that we are, in fact, getting what we want. James Kincaid (2004) pinpoints this problem in his study of the erotic child who—vacant—awaits our occupancy:

> The construction of the "modern" child is very largely an evacuation, the ruthless sending out of eviction notices. Correspondingly, the instructions we receive on what to regard as sexually arousing tell us to look for (and often create) this emptiness, to discover the erotic in that which is most susceptible to inscription, the blank page. On that page we can write what we like, write it and then long for it, love it, have it. Children are defined, and longed for, according to what *they* do not have. (10)

This child is both empty and full—emptied so she can be filled. Understood almost entirely in relation to adult desires, "the child" is caught between sexuality and knowledge, between defense and wish. Within queer theory, writing on "the child" picks up these contradictions. Michael Cobb (2005) puts it this way: "Children can be most anything, other than themselves. And because they are pressured to do the work of placeholders for so much political, cultural, affective activity, they are everywhere, and they're very important" (119).

Lee Edelman makes this claim most powerfully in his polemic, *No Future*. Edelman claims that queerness throws into relief the cultural and political work we expect "the child" to do. He asserts there is no such thing as a queer child; the queer child is not a child at all. According to Edelman, "the child"—as figure, as idealization, as promise—stands against the possibility of homosexuality entering politics as queerness. "For the cult of the Child permits no shrines to the queerness of boys and girls, since queerness . . . is understood as bringing children and childhood to an end" (2004, 19). Capitalizing the Child to indicate its status as a concept, Edelman argues that the Child, constructed as "the future," is at the center of all politics, left and right. If the Child "remains the perpetual horizon of every acknowledged politics," then "queerness names the side of those *not* 'fighting for the children,' the side outside the consensus by which all politics confirms the absolute value of reproductive futurism" (3). For Edelman, "reproductive futurism" describes how the Child is positioned as the future and therefore as the justification for all political thought and action.

Here, queerness stands at a remove from those identities we name as gay, lesbian, bisexual, and transgender. As LGBTQ adults work to bring their lost childhoods into the fold by narrating a coherent story of development, queerness embodies a radical, nonutilitarian possibility: an outside to oppositional politics. And because all identity—even the gay kind—is oppositional (I am this and not that), queerness is a refusal to participate in a fantasy of becoming, when the self is imagined as the future unfolding. For Edelman, queerness is not an identity but a quality of experience, a reading practice, a position, or an aesthetic orientation.

No Future offers a provocation to reimagine a queer politics that would find its ground in something other than the promise of a better future and all the attendant reproductive hopes that accompany those dreams—and provoke it has. Serving as one touchstone for the renewal of queer theory, *No Future* has received praise and critique from all corners of the queer academic world, particularly for what is seen as its embrace of a radical political negativity and what gets called its antirelational or antisocial thesis. If queer theory is not about imagining better futures, if it is not organized around the possibility of a radical hope, then, critics ask, how can we avoid falling into political nihilism? Can sexuality produce a politics or a pedagogy? Or, as Edelman argues, does sexuality push against and disturb dreams of sociality, solidarity, and transformation? These questions concern both how sexual identities will become legible in legal and political contexts and the more ordinary problem of how young people will be called into queer communities. For Edelman, "the child" houses all of the compromised political dreams in which access to a happy, queer life is possible on the condition that we, too, take up and invest in the currency of reproductive futurism.

"The child," according to Edelman, is defined partly as an antonym to queerness. But, as part of this ongoing debate, recent writing on the queer child pushes back against Edelman, conceding his point that children have been appropriated as political capital, but then excavating intimacies between the queer and the child. Echoing the language of overdetermination, Stockton (2009) calls the queer child "a dense configuration" (278). This density marries the queer to the child: "Queers, one observes, trail children behind them or alongside them, as if they are wedded, one to another, in unforeseen ways. This interests me. But so does the seeming flip side of this axiom. Scratch a child, you will find a queer" (278–79). The queer child, which Stockton recognizes as describing both the queer's childness and the child's queerness, augurs hope. Turning to a range of literary texts, Stockton describes the queer child growing sideways and, in this twist, signals her critique of normative developmental models. If children grow up, then we adults are always standing on top of them. Sideways growth implies horizontal rather than vertical change—shifts, slides, substitutions. For Stockton, these are the movements of metaphor, where meanings slip from one term to another, and this instability opens up new places for thinking. The queer child, as a figure for metaphor, can never be pinned down. She is an antinominalization; always just out of grasp, the queer child is incoherent even as she is saturated with meaning.

This queer child figured by Edelman and Stockton stands uneasily beside "the child," pushing back against that child's promise of an empty innocence. As I shift to a discussion of two court cases, where "the child"—decidedly not queer even if LGBTQ—is central to debates over LGBTQ rights, I trace how a queerness haunts those proceedings. Even as these cases make strong arguments for the expansion of LGBTQ rights, they are saturated with fantasies of worlds without ambiguity, hatred, or difference, and the cases must disavow the presence of an unsettling queerness—the possibility that childhoods do not predict adulthoods and that queer sexuality, if untethered from the verticality of development, may not settle down into legible LGBTQ identities.

Making the Case

A certain version of childhood looms large in the constitution of adult LGBTQ sexualities. The child we once were, or hoped we might have been, figures strongly in narratives of gay, lesbian, and transgender adult identities.[3] Here is one example, taken from the blog of transgender singer Lucas Silveira:

> When I was four, and in a childhood moment of absolute innocence, after having seen my brothers at bath time, I asked my mother to buy me a penis like his. Why had I not been bought one? She of course laughed and said that I was a girl and girls don't have a penis. A normal response from a parent. I was devastated. Well, this moment was the first of a struggle I endured until two and a half years ago. I lived my entire childhood and adolescent life knowing that I was in the wrong body. But who had words to explain what I was going through? Who was like me? Nobody. I felt alone. I thought I was alone. I thought I was mentally ill. I could never tell a soul.[4]

This story of lonely development is deeply painful and ubiquitous. Who hasn't felt different as a child? Who hasn't located the source of some adult predilection in the innocent question of our former child self? In our adult stories of identity, our child selves are always asking precocious questions that crack open the punishing logic of social norms. These children arrive before their time and call our adult selves into existence. Stockton calls this presence the ghostly gay child. The metaphor of the ghost suggests the untimeliness of this child—prescient and late. The ghostly gay child carries the hint of a future. He will grow up into his queerness. But the ghostly gay child is only ever recognized after that growing has happened, after words and names and labels have replaced an inarticulate but felt presence. Stockton terms this strange chronology the "backward birth" of the queer child (2009, 6). In his narrative of childhood difference, Silveira's transgender self is birthed backward and the origin story gathers its force in the afterwardness of development.

It may be impossible to conceptualize adulthood on anything other than the ontological bedrock of childhood. But when LGBTQ adults insist on locating the origins of our sexual or gender identity in childhood—so that development looks like a long, straight march into the inevitable—we prop up a version of "the child" that is understood only in relation to its futurity. Far from being a purely theoretical problem, the construction of the child as the origin of the adult—gay, straight, or transgender—undergirds the equality-seeking claims of LGBTQ communities as much as it does the conservative, "family values" backlash against those claims. And, insofar as both groups create the child who must be saved—children are the future / we are the future of our childhoods—we remain in an ideological deadlock. We must ask, therefore, what we want and need from "the child" in the name of education, or in the name of a LGBTQ politics. That is, how do our pedagogical and political efforts to inculcate tolerance, for instance, invent both the subject who must learn to tolerate difference and the subject who must be tolerated? These debates intersect with educational and legal conflicts over the status of the child and childhoods. Our capacity to theorize childhood as something more than the projection of adult desires onto smaller bodies is central to an LGBTQ politics that could open itself up to the indirection/misdirection of desire and to a pedagogy that can tolerate the child's estrangement from forms of adult subjectivity. That is, if politics could be touched by queer theory, we must risk holding stories of development open for sideways growth.

Two Canadian court cases each battle over "the child" in a fight to protect and advance the civil rights of LGBTQ individuals. In the first, *Chamberlain v. Surrey School District*, a local school board tried to ban as inappropriate picture books that depict a range of families, including same-sex families. In the second, *Nixon v. Vancouver Rape Relief Society*, a transsexual woman was barred from volunteering at a rape crisis center on the grounds that she had lived her childhood as a boy. In each case the child is figured as the vulnerable origin of the adult who must be protected from conflict so that her adult identity, whether straight, gay, or transsexual, could emerge from childhood experience. Both of these cases have been important touchstones in Canada for testing the equality claims of LGBTQ communities. These cases draw on a history of legal discourse and jurisprudence that has recognized and gradually expanded the civil rights of LGBTQ individuals while also defining what it means to be both LGBTQ and a Canadian citizen.[5] My argument focuses less on the outcomes of these cases or even their importance in Canadian human rights jurisprudence and more on how each case makes a link between claims for equality and the experience of childhood. When human and civil rights for LGBTQ people are conceptualized as adult issues, the queer adult nevertheless needs "the child" in order to advance her claim for civil rights, and those opposing the expansion of civil rights also need "the child" as an alibi for their continuing discrimination.

Early in 1997, in Surrey, British Columbia (BC), a conservative suburb of Vancouver, James Chamberlain requested permission from his local school board to use three picture books in his kindergarten and grade-one classes to supplement the Personal Planning / Family Life Education curriculum. Chamberlain, a gay teacher, hoped to offer his students a broader representation of families—blended families, mixed-faith and -race families, single-parent families, and lesbian- and gay-headed families. The three books he chose—*Asha's Mums* (1990) by Rosamund Elwin and Michelle Paulse, *Belinda's Bouquet* (1991) by Leslea Newman, and *One Dad, Two Dads, Brown Dads, Blue Dads* (1994) by Johnny Valentine—all depict a same-sex family as part of the story. Read today, more than twenty years after their initial publication, these books feel anything but controversial—indeed, they adopt a rather hygienic tone. The political desire to represent lesbian- and gay-headed families as normal and loving trumps literari- ness.[6] Yet now—as then—a picture of a little boy proclaiming his love for his gay dad has the potential to cause outrage. As Lorraine Weir (2003), academic and expert witness for Chamberlain in the case, argues, it is the "depiction" of lesbian and gay families that is understood as obscene. Picture books are dangerous precisely because they put pictures in children's heads: as the school board argued, "The representation of lesbians and gays as 'normal' could give young people the wrong idea" (29).[7] So, in the spring of 1997, the Surrey District School Board passed a resolution prohib- iting the three books from being used in the classroom, arguing that the books might introduce a religious conflict between what children are taught at home and what they are taught at school. The board passed this resolution despite receiving a petition from seventeen of twenty families in Chamberlain's class supporting the use of these books.

That summer, five people, including Chamberlain and James Warren, teacher and founder of the Gay and Lesbian Educators (GALE) of BC, filed suit against the Surrey District School Board in the BC Supreme Court claiming that their rights to equality and freedom of expression had been violated by the book ban. The lawsuit, supported by lesbian and gay communities across Canada, became known as the "Bigots Ban Books" case. The BC Supreme Court agreed with that characterization and in Decem- ber 1998 issued a decision overturning the ban. The school board appealed, and in the fall of 2000 the BC Court of Appeal unani- mously reversed the BC Supreme Court ruling and—citing the International Covenant on Civil and Political Rights—argued that there needs to be "respect for the liberty of parents to ensure the religious and moral education of their children in conformity with their own convictions."

In 2002 the Supreme Court of Canada agreed to hear the appeal, and in June both sides brought their case to Ottawa. Six months later, the court ruled in favor of Chamberlain and his co-plaintiffs. In her 7-2 decision for the majority, Chief Justice Beverly McLaughlin found that the school board's decision to prohibit the use of these books was unreasonable. Sidestepping constitutional issues and basing their decision in administrative law, the court found that the school has a responsibility to consider the perspectives of religious and nonreligious parents, but also that schools have a responsibility to promote values of tolerance and diversity and to protect the children of lesbian and gay parents.

The second case began in August 1995 when Kimberly Nixon began attending a training course for volunteer crisis counselors at the Vancouver Rape Relief Society (VRRS). During the first session, one of the facilitators suspected that Nixon was a transsexual woman and approached Nixon to confirm her suspicions. When asked if she was born a man, Nixon answered yes. With this disclosure, VRRS found Nixon unfit to be a volunteer on the crisis line. VRRS defines itself as a woman-only organization, and according to the organization, although Kimberly Nixon may be a woman in many senses, even the legal sense, her experience growing up as a boy disqualifies her from the identity of "woman" as the organization defines it. Nixon, herself a survivor of male-partner violence, found this exclusion extremely hurtful; while she was woman enough to be a victim of male-partner violence and woman enough to be helped by organizations devoted to supporting battered women, VRRS insisted she was not woman enough to counsel other victims. By refusing to allow her to train as a volunteer counselor, VRRS implicitly marked Nixon as a potential threat to other women. In statements made to the media, spokeswomen for VRRS insisted that the sight of Nixon could be enough to cause harm to women accessing their services.

That year, Nixon, along with longtime queer rights activist and attorney barbara findlay, filed a complaint with the BC Human

Rights Commission. The case was not heard by the tribunal until late 2000. The commission had a backlog of cases that stalled their investigation, and the VRRS went to provincial court to have the tribunal dismissed because of institutional delay; they also argued, more perniciously, that gender identity was not yet protected by the BC Human Rights Code. The judge disagreed, and the case went before the tribunal which, after hearing arguments for several months, decided in favor of Nixon and awarded her seventy-five hundred dollars as compensation for hurt feelings.

The case did not stop there. In August 2003 the BC Supreme Court conducted a judicial review of the case and concluded that the tribunal had erred; the court found that VRRS did not discriminate against Nixon and did have the right to exclude transsexual women from its organization. The court refused to send the case back to the tribunal, and Nixon appealed to the BC Court of Appeal. The Court of Appeal upheld the BC Supreme Court ruling. Nixon then appealed to the Supreme Court of Canada, her last avenue, but the Court declined to hear her case.

Both of these cases rest on the backs of childhoods—real and imagined. Despite their anteriority to LGBTQ civil rights, arguments in both cases conjured up scenes of children hurt by LGBTQ rights and by trans- and homophobia. In *Nixon v. Vancouver Rape Relief Society*, the relation between the child and the adult is reconstructive as Kimberly Nixon's childhood becomes the contested grounds of her exclusion from VRRS *and* the grounds for her inclusion. VRRS claims that Nixon's experience living her childhood as a boy means that she is not qualified to counsel women through the trauma of male violence. In response, Nixon argues that even as a child she was never a boy and that her corrected birth certificate now records her true sex, female. Both sides of the argument draw a substantial link between the child one was and the adult one becomes. Commentary on the case has focused on the problematic construction of "experience" as the grounds of knowledge (cf. Namaste 2005)—a debate that is well rehearsed in education as well—but more difficult is the positioning of childhood experience as the direct source of a stable adult identity.

In *Chamberlain v. Surrey School District*, "the child" was the legal battleground. Arguments for both sides of the case summoned up powerful images of children injured by their education: children of LGBTQ families need to be protected from discrimination, children of conservative heterosexual families need to be protected from the conflict of seeing alternative versions of family, and children who will one day grow up to become gay or lesbian need their self-esteem protected from negative stereotypes of lesbians and gays. In each of these worries, there is a confidence that education, when not a source of conflict, can direct children toward the kind of adulthoods we might want for them. And, in an echo of the Nixon case, children must carry the burden of adults' fantasies for the future.

Queer Childhoods

In the Chamberlain case, the three contested books for primary students are meant to introduce students to the different configurations that families might take: stepfamilies, extended families, mixed-race families, divorced families, single-parent families, and most controversially, same-sex families. Talking about same-sex families in primary school means acknowledging that some students may have gay or lesbian parents, or uncles or aunts. This curriculum asks that teachers acknowledge that students' experiences of family are diverse. What the curriculum cannot say, and what the emphasis on gays and lesbians as parents occludes, is the contradictory relationship that children may have to the possibility of queerness. It is radical to insist, as Chamberlain does, that some children may become gays and lesbians themselves. Even if gay and lesbian adults enjoy civil rights, there is no way to conceptualize becoming gay or lesbian outside of pathology or a sense that one has gone awry. Or, more poignantly in the Nixon case, there is no way to conceptualize a boy becoming a woman except to argue that either one was never a boy or one is not really a woman. If there are no manuals on how to bring your kids up gay, there are certainly no manuals on how to bring your boys up to be women. But, as difficult as it is to see students in the first grade as future gays, lesbians, or transgender people, the more difficult possibility is not conceptualizing "the child" as the future unfolding, no matter if the future is queer. What gets lost in the claiming of queer childhoods are those childhoods that either aren't marked as queer or don't foreshadow a queer adulthood. The femme girl or the sporty boy whose gender presentation seemingly matches up with social norms is abandoned to hetero-normativity: How might their queer childhoods be told? And what of the children of LGBTQ parents—who affectionately call themselves "queer spawn": How can their relationship to the promise of queerness find room within these normative trajectories?

The political and pedagogical challenge is to disentangle tolerance for LGBTQ people from the fantasy of a queer future. In this fantasy, the utterance "I was a gay child" marks the death of a straight person and retroactively creates a coming-of-age narrative that secures one's experience in childhood to an always already existing identity (Stockton 2004, 283). When the child stands in for the future, she embodies the ideal of identity without loss and uncertainty. Within this logic, the precocious questions of childhood lose their interrogative quality, and instead questions forecast answers about the future. In this paradigm, there is no estrangement, no conflict, and no loss that cannot be repaired through the consolidation of an adult LGBTQ identity. Yet the quality of experience that Edelman calls "queerness" emerges from loss and the inconsolable gap between desire and identity—where who I am and what I want do not lie flush with each other. To return to Wiegman's (2012) axiom, "It is impossible to know in advance how anyone will need to travel the distance between her desires and the world in which those desires must (try to) live" (159). This impossibility disrupts the anticipatory routes from childhoods to adulthoods.

However, in these court cases, in narratives of coming out and in the conservative use of "the child" in antigay politics, the idealized child—the child as future—is innocent, untainted by the rupture between desire and identity, and has therefore not yet lost anything. From this vantage point where "the child" is centered, all politics becomes locked into a conservative logic that defends against loss by finding its justification in betterment, a sense of promise, and redemption. As Silviera's story suggests, there is a straight, if bumpy, line from the "innocent" question of a child to the articulation of a transgender identity. This logic constructs history as progress and forecloses the possibility of imagining other modes of being in time, including the radical possibility that sexuality (or childhood) as queerness is both before and beyond identity and therefore knows no time.

These arguments about the theoretical status of the child can feel estranged from our everyday efforts to establish kind, loving, and meaningful conditions in which children can grow up. It matters, of course, that James Chamberlain's fight against the censorship of the school board was successful and that transgender people continue to face widespread state-sponsored discrimination both in their exclusion from human rights legislation and in everyday acts of administrative injustice (Spade 2011). I want to argue also that the grounds of our arguments for the full and robust inclusion of LGBTQ people in public life matter for the future of those fights. In our efforts to imagine a vigorous LGBTQ politic, we must also wonder what work we make our theoretical children perform—how narratives of childhood constructed by adults, as a justification for adulthood, come to affect our understanding of real, live children whose speech and actions may conflict with those narrative fantasies on which we rely. And even if, as I have been arguing, the use of "the child" in stories of LGBTQ identities rescues the ghostly gay child and restores to him his tarnished innocence, these fights over the children remind us that despite the enormous advances in human rights made by LGBTQ communities, queerness—whenever it arrives—is greeted ambivalently. If LGBTQ communities have sought to look back and rescue their childhoods by bringing them into significance, this resuscitation is done against a backdrop of continuing neglect, pathologization, and even hatred. It may be a conservative move on the part of LGBTQ communities, but there is also a felt need that something needs to be conserved. As Eve Sedgwick (1993) notes, "I think everyone who does gay and lesbian studies is haunted by the suicides of adolescents" (1). The metaphor of haunting names the loss that makes identity: what will have been said about me was that I survived.

Could we instead give the child space and time to grow into whatever—to see her being as important as her becoming? It may seem like a difficult time to insist that we leave the child alone. As the two cases remind us, education is charged with the important task of crafting a generous and open language to address the infinite ways people may choose to live in their bodies and in relation to others. It may be too easy to simply insert gays and lesbians into normative narratives of the family, or to rely on normative discourses of development to tie the boy to the woman. But conversely, it is also too easy to declare "the family" bankrupt, to abandon efforts to have the human and civil rights of LGBTQ communities fully recognized by the state. To confront the flurry of anxieties and desires that coalesce around expanding rights for LGBTQ students and families in education, we need to notice how narratives of "the child"—no matter if gay—forget and defend against the queerness that sexuality might become. If queerness is not to be collapsed into identity and so become a quality of experience available to anyone, education must be open to the surprise of sideways growth so that we can learn to tolerate that we can be nothing or anything.

2 THERE IS NO SUCH THING AS AN ADOLESCENT

Sex Education as Taking a Risk

SEX EDUCATION RESTS ON A DISTINCTION between adults and adolescents. Who is the subject of sex education? Whose sexuality is in need of education? To put the question differently: Who is the adolescent in need of sex education, and who is the adult distinguished from the adolescent, in part, by not needing sex education? While we are accustomed to seeing the adolescent as requiring an adult, both for its construction as a historical, social, and psychological category, and in the ordinary sense that adults provide support for the social and psychological work of growing up through adolescence, we are less accustomed to considering how the adult needs the adolescent. Yet this relation of nonrelation—the repudiation of the adolescent who lives on in the adult—is the underside of sex education, defended against thorough assertions of pedagogical authority, assertions that forget the impossibility of positioning oneself as an "expert on sex" (Phillips 1997, 89). For this nonrelation to be available for thinking, rather than forgetting, we might take Simon Watney's (1991) advice and "invert the usual question of what children supposedly want or need from education, and ask what it is that adults want from children in the name of 'education'" (398).

The pedagogical relationship between the adult and the adolescent is the focus of the next three chapters. In what ways do youth need adults to move through the developmental tasks of adolescence? And, echoing the discussion of "the child" in chapter 1, how do adults lean on their own remembered adolescences while working with contemporary youth? This relationship is the subject of much critical study in education. Researchers critique how youth, in relation to adults, are socially constructed as deficient, dangerous, in need of protection, or caught in time (cf. Fields 2008; Fine 1988; Lesko 2001; Pillow 2004). In championing the interests of youth, this work insists on young people's humanity, capacity for love and pleasure, and ability to take responsibility for their own and their partners' bodies. Indeed, these powerful critiques ask the radical question: What would it mean for adults to see adolescents as sexual subjects, and as having a right to experience the risks of sexuality, while also recognizing adults' responsibility to create the conditions for thoughtfulness, care, and curiosity both in and out of schools?

The challenge of this question is that it requires adults to consider our own perceptions of youth and to place youth in relation to our views of sexuality, maturity, and vague, largely unarticulated beliefs about "grownupness." In the next three chapters I take up this challenge and try to describe some of the contours of "grownupness," a territory that rests uncertainly on the experiences, wishes, and ideas of real and imagined adolescences. The relation that must be risked, I argue, is not just the relation between adult and youth but within the adult herself, since working with youth has the potential to call into crisis our tentative claim to adulthood. The psychoanalyst D. W. Winnicott, who serves as a trusted guide in this chapter, appreciates the challenge that youth pose to the adults' sense of self. His inclination is to see adults, rather than youth, as needing support to survive what he calls the adolescent doldrums. He reminds us, "If we are talking about adolescence, we are talking about adults, because no adults are all the time adult. This is because people are not just their own age; they are to some extent every age, or no age" (1984, 137). This advice is particularly important for those who work in sex education, where the distinction between youth and adults can become ossified, not just by those adults who refuse to see youth as capable of enjoying healthy sexual lives, but also by adults and youth alike who may harden "youth" into a category divorced from the disappointments and pleasures of adulthood.

To imagine youth as sexual subjects, we need to have a theory of adolescent sexuality, how it differs from and is similar to adult sexuality; further, we need to have a patience and curiosity about the ways that adult sexuality is inhabited by the memories, fantasies, and experiences of adolescence. That is, sex education must make room for a theory of adolescence without casting the adolescent in the risky role of not yet adult. Julia Kristeva (1990) blurs the epistemological distinction between the adult and adolescent and considers "the term 'adolescent' less an age category than an open psychic structure" (8). Such an orientation requires us to abandon the wish that adolescence ends with adulthood or that youth is only a social convention; instead, I argue that adolescence, and also therefore adulthood, is a psychical relation.

Thinking about sex education and sexuality through the problem of relationality opens up the well-guarded distinction between adolescence as a social and historical construction and adolescence as a biological or physiological event. In the often dreary fights between social constructivism and essentialism, development becomes either a description of adolescent experience or, more perniciously, a means to govern youth's bodies. This myopia forecloses the more radical possibility that "development" be understood as an effect of the contested relations between adults and adolescents, as well as the conflicts within the self. Precisely this relationality is repudiated in the debates around social constructivism and essentialism; the adolescent becomes either a problem of social convention or an effect of an unruly physiology or psychology, and the adult escapes unscathed. Sex education, through a reliance on the terms of the nature–culture debate, perpetuates this splitting, inventing the youth who require an education and the adults who, by virtue of their grownupness, have escaped the emotional risks of sexuality.

This view is supported by Britzman (1998a), who notes the paucity of models for thinking about sex education. She names three categories: the normal, which adopts a normative physiological or psychological theory of adolescence; the critical, which treats adolescence as a social construction and a problem of identity; and the one not yet tolerated, which is not tolerated precisely because sexuality is conceptualized as a relation that is not reducible to either biology or identity (66). Much important contemporary thinking in sex education falls into the critical category (cf. Elliott 2012; Fields 2008; Fine 1988; Lesko 2010; Irvine 2002). In this work attention is paid to how the adolescent is constructed through discourses of history, culture, class, race, gender, and ability. In her study of parents' understandings of their teenage children's sex lives, Sinikka Elliott (2012), for instance, argues that parents are able to maintain the illusion of their teens' sexual innocence as long as there are other teens—usually racialized— available to be cast as corrupting influences. In this research, the universal concept of "the adolescent" is undone by an attention to how social formations shape a young person's experience of sexuality.

These critiques malign sex education for reproducing a normative adolescent who meets and confirms each stage of development and imagine sex education as a new emancipatory space for young people to critically examine the social construction of sexuality (Fields 2008). How then, in the face of this powerful critique, to bring a cautious theory of development to our conversations about sex education? Handled gingerly, theories of development can also be narratives about the psychical relations that create the adolescent. With this lens, sex education is larger than information, affirmation, or prohibition. In its address to the most intimate aspects of life—love, loss, vulnerability, power, friendship, aggression—sex education is necessarily entangled in the youth's efforts to construct a self, find love outside the family, and enjoy a newly adult body—in short, various relationships that might cautiously be called developmental.

I want to make a claim for a cautious theory of development in sex education. The theory must be cautious because "development" has an uneven history in educational thought. According to Erik Erikson (1963), himself a theorist of development, when theories of development meet the imperatives of education, they move too quickly from tools for thinking to tools for measuring and correcting—a shift that critical studies of sex education rightly condemn. My argument, like Erikson's, is grounded in psychoanalysis and the interpretive possibilities that are opened up when a good life is measured not by one's proximity to norms but by one's capacity to love and work—themselves risky occupations (Freud 1930). Sex education as well, I argue, might be oriented toward the risks of love and work.

Sex education and theories of adolescence have long been preoccupied with the concept of "risk." Spanning the 1983 publication of *A Nation at Risk*, a report that wedded youth to "risk"; continuing with the educational response to the AIDS pandemic; and now finding new life in discussions about LGBTQ bullying, the concept of risk hovers around youth and their perceived proximity to danger. This is a stark example of what Linda Singer (1993, 29) calls "an epidemic logic"; risk may be seen to arise from bullying, for instance, but it migrates easily from harassment to suicide to academic underachievement to homelessness. In these slippery moves, risk is anywhere and nowhere. As theorists of HIV/AIDS education first noticed, and as an "epidemic logic" demonstrates, risk is not merely the perception of an objective hazard but also a state of feeling (Odets 1995; Patton 1996; Britzman 1998b; White 1999). Here, risk is not only a danger in the outside world, it is also a condition of being; the very sense of riskiness or being "at risk" can come from the difficulty of deciding whether risk originates in the outside world or emanates from internal reality. As psychoanalysts Joseph Sandler and D. W. Winnicott each argue, taking risks can be a way to feel alive, even if those risks put the self in danger. We must therefore ask in sex education: What or where are the risks of adolescence? Moreover, we must do so without immediately positing youth as a group "at risk." Such a question requires that we see risk not as a zero-sum game but as a condition of development, as part of the sideways work of growing up. To understand risk—and adolescence—not as an objective hazard, but as a quality of interior life, we need to revisit our interpretations of risk-taking in sex education. Indeed, as I argue throughout this chapter, rather than trying to extricate youth from risk, for adolescence to occur, a risk must be taken. But tolerating this view of adolescence as development requires something more of adults and sex educators: the risk of relationality.

Developmental Problems

"Development" has come into disfavor among critical theorists in education, and for good reason. Developmental psychology relies on a discourse of development that categorizes and measures children and adolescents according to their increasing social, emotional, and cognitive abilities. In positioning the normative as the ideal, if fictional, center of developmental theory, children and youth are monitored according to their proximity to or distance from that ideal.

The effects of this logic are insidious. Jonathan Silin (1995) argues that this insistence on the linearity of development creates an unbridgeable gap between children and adults: "the accomplishment of adulthood appears to be ever more complex and far from the haunts of early childhood" (104). By positioning adulthood as an accomplishment, developmental theory constructs children and youth as deficient and not yet fully human. Adults may have once been children and then adolescent, but most often the implications of this intimate history for the present fall outside the scope of developmental theory. According to Jacqueline Rose (1992):

> Childhood is part of a strict developmental sequence at the end of which stands the cohered and rational consciousness of the adult mind. Children may, on occasion, be disturbed, but they do not disturb us as long as that sequence (and that development) can be ensured. Children are no threat to our identity because they are,

so to speak, "on their way" (the journey metaphor is a recurrent one). Their difference stands purely as a sign of just how far we have progressed. (13)

Rose insists that the child of developmental theory is not only a reflection of our constructions of childhood but also a measure of adulthood. We cannot feel secure in our grownupness and feel that we have arrived at adulthood without the figure of the dependent and helpless child.

It may seem odd to turn to Erik Erikson for commentary on this issue. In critiques of developmentalism, his important essay "The Eight Ages of Man" is often scorned for reducing maturation to the eight "stages" of man. But Erikson himself cautioned against reading his work as offering a predictable set of vertical stages that the child must pass through on the way to adulthood. Erikson held out his greatest caution for educators, who in their enthusiasm for testing might make development a pass-or-fail exam. The final footnote in his essay reads:

> The assumption that on each stage [of the eight ages] a goodness is achieved which is impervious to new inner conflicts and to changing conditions is, I believe, a projection in child development of that success ideology which can so dangerously pervade our private and public daydreams and can make us inept in a heightened struggle for a meaningful existence. (1963, 274)

Developmental theory, as both Rose and Erikson argue, is an effect of the conflicts between the experiences and struggles of children and the wishes and projections of adults. The hierarchies and binaries that developmental theory relies on are of little use to children or adolescents but may describe, albeit symptomatically, the experience and disappointment of having grown up—our ineptitude when faced with the struggle to create a meaningful existence.

Rather than understand development as this struggle for a meaningful existence, the dominance of universal and linear theories of development in education connects growing up to an achievement. In these theories, the child cannot help but be pulled into the progressive capabilities of adulthood, yet sex education offers us a different view of development. While developmental theory is seen as the grounds of pedagogical practice (Silin 1995, 87), the anxieties that surround the role of sex education in schools reveal an abiding fear of precocity. If development is conceptualized as a set of steps leading from childhood up to adulthood, sex education exposes the underside of that confidence: we might arrive too early or come too late. The most common pedagogical questions in sex education acknowledge the fragility of this trajectory. We ask: What are the most efficient ways to discourage adolescents from engaging in premarital/precocious sexual activity? For instance, we ask: How can we teach youth to use condoms every time they have sexual intercourse? How can we promote the value of long-lasting monogamous relationships? How can we instill in youth an esteem for their own and their partner's well-being and health? These questions, however, belie a more fundamental concern: What is sexuality that it might easily go astray or arrive too early or too often? What makes sexuality susceptible, or not, to outside influence? Is it sexuality that puts the self at risk, or are there other ways to conceptualize its meanings?

Here is where psychoanalysis offers a different language of development that is helpful for sex education. For psychoanalysis, sexuality inaugurates, rather than ruins, subjectivity, but this inauguration can only be known later, after the event. Our sense of development emerges in what Laplanche (1992, 217) translates as the "afterwardness" of experience: we will tell the story of adolescence from the blinkered vantage point of adulthood. In this view, theories of development are not simply a description of adolescent experience but are an effect of adults' ambivalence toward youth. Psychoanalytic theories of development begin with this conflict and the assumption that each developmental "achievement" is made from a loss that, while necessary, places the self in jeopardy. Instead of seeing adolescence as a dilemma of precocity, the key questions look backward: In what ways is growing up also a giving up? What are the costs of adulthood, maturity, or identity? The orientation is reconstructive rather than prescriptive or prophylactic. The story of development is told backward. As Juliet Mitchell (2000) explains:

> Freud was listening to the recollected history of his patients, he reconstructed infantile life from the fragmentary stories the patient told in which time past and time present are one. He read the history of the person backwards—as it is always essential to do; but in retelling it, he describes it as a march forward where it is in fact a multi-level effort at reconstruction. (14)

This narrative of development as reconstruction loses its predictive promise, but psychoanalysis compensates by opening up new interpretive vantage points. Experience is not what happened, but how; in the afterwardness of reconstruction, history becomes what Lisa Farley (2011) calls "the labor of the negative"—the capacity to "tolerate the absences, displacements and deferrals of meaning that exceed what the 'facts' can tell" (11). What gets called experience, then, is an effect of this untimely historical process.

With this understanding of development, interpretation comes too late to save adults from the difficulties of their own adolescence. Nonetheless, it is exactly this work of interpretation, making meaning, and constructing persuasive narratives of love and loss that is at stake in sex education (Casemore, Sandlos, and Gilbert 2011). If sex education places the problem of interpretation and relationality at the center of its mandate, then the challenge for the adult is to tolerate "the absences, displacements and deferrals of meaning" that constitute their own adolescent history while also understanding adolescent risk-taking as a symptom of developmental work and an aspect of what Winnicott (1986) calls adolescents' "immaturity" (160).

There Is No Such Thing As an Adolescent

Winnicott can act as a compassionate guide into the dilemmas of youth. His commitment is first of all to a theory of adolescent development that refuses to harden the distinctions between youth and adults. Winnicott recognizes that one's sense of self emerges through our often conflicted and ambivalent relationships with others. In a now infamous statement, Winnicott (1992) declares—"rather excitedly and with some heat: *'thing as a baby'*. . . . If you show me a baby you certainly show me also someone caring for the baby, or at least a pram with someone's eyes and ears glued to it" (99). For Winnicott (1989a), the baby cannot be extricated from what he names "the facilitating environment" (139), those material, maternal, and psychical conditions of care that allow the baby room for experience. The baby, therefore, only exists within the context of its care, nurturance, attention from others, and so on. For the baby, the failure of the facilitating environment to provide adequate care is not only physically debilitating but psychically disintegrating. In this way, poverty, hunger, and neglect (as well as love, warmth, and attention) are psychical experiences (and resources) for the baby. Winnicott's insistence that there is no such thing as a baby dissolves the stark divisions of interior and exterior, nature and culture, and the separation of child from adult. For Winnicott, you cannot understand babies without understanding parents.

I want to follow Winnicott's logic and suggest that there is no such thing as an adolescent. If you show me an adolescent, you certainly also show me parents, teachers, friends and peer groups, school, police, the fashion industry, the media, the mall, and so on. These figures and institutions constitute a facilitating environment for adolescent development or, more particularly, for the adolescent to use as he or she goes about the work of growing up. For Winnicott, development does not end with the end of childhood: adolescence is a difficult time because one is living the history of their early development even as one is facing new developmental tasks. And, like the baby who comes into a family that is ordinarily fraught with conflict, the adolescent grows up through the parents' ambivalence toward their children and the their own ambivalence toward their parents.

Certain developmental experiences are associated with youth—crafting an identity; making a relationship to one's changing body; using language to order experience, the self, and others; falling in love with oneself and others. In psychoanalysis, these experiences are part of the painful work of giving up the parents as love objects. At times this work feels more like throwing away, denigration, or absolute indifference (to the parents especially), but the intensity of these aggressive and hostile defenses suggests the enormity of the task. Freud would describe these relations as Oedipal to indicate that the child's psychical life is bound up in their relationship to their parents. In adolescence, the Oedipal narrative that Freud uses to describe the emotional lives of infants and children once again comes to the fore. Relationships with parents and parent substitutes (including teachers) are subject to the extremes of love and hate, derision and neediness, and idealization and disparagement. The Oedipal narrative is a story of passion, but it is also a story of loss and its compensations. To become adults, youth must give up passionate attachments to parents. But these attachments live on in the subject: the lost object that represents early infantile love is internalized as authority—Freud (1923, 36) names the superego as the heir to the Oedipal complex—and sexual identity, or the consolidation of sexuality with authority.

The internalization of authority in adolescence finds its origins in infancy when love first becomes entangled in authority and helplessness. Eventually, the child realizes that being loved comes with conditions. The child's awareness of her exclusion from her parents' relationship is the first great loss. Kaplan (1984) describes the conflict well: "The Oedipal scenario is the culmination of the infantile legend of losing libidinal objects. It does, however, produce a gain of sorts. In exchange for her loss the child acquires as her own some inner authority to rule over her own desires" (122). The child cannot have the parents as love objects and so instead she takes this prohibition inside and internalizes the parents' sense of authority. Indeed, our first love becomes the love of authority, institutionalized in the superego.

This history of losing love and gaining a sense of authority is ambivalent, and in adolescence, when fights with authority figure prominently, this volatile history is reenacted. Winnicott suggests that when there is a fight with authority (and he was speaking specifically of juvenile delinquency), there has been a loss, what he calls "a deprivation" (Winnicott 1986, 91). This dynamic is important to consider in sex education. Sex education is normally structured around appeals to authority, and the success of programs is often measured through compliance. These appeals take at least three forms. First, adult authority may be insisted on through campaigns that admonish youth to "just say no" to sex. Second, youths' reliance on the external authority of group norms is appealed to. The goal is to make using condoms a group norm (or in the case of virginity pledges, to make abstinence a group norm). Third, sex education targets youths' internal sense of authority through appeals to the superego. These campaigns tell youth to take care of their body, take responsibility for their actions, and so on. However, the superego can be surprisingly harsh, and thus this appeal to one's conscience is apt to incite feelings of persecution and guilt, two states that are especially impervious to the address of sex education. The difficulty in each of these three cases is that youth's relationships with authority are ambivalent—love and hate, conformity and rebellion commingle in a volatile mixture of friendship, hero worship, and repudiation—and therefore, whenever we appeal to youth's sense of authority, we are conjuring up an unstable and psychically combustible dynamic. Indeed, any demand made of youth in the name of authority, internal or external, runs the risk of inciting a concomitant acting out.

I want to suggest that these fights with authority can be interpreted as an effect of Oedipal conflict. And while the language of the Oedipal may seem excessively literal, the dilemmas of Oedipal conflict are experienced as ordinary and familiar: the adolescent yearns for independence, finds solace in the acceptance of peer groups, hates his or her parents, and grows nostalgic for the lost innocence of childhood. This task of leaving one's parents behind to invent new selves Kristeva (2000) calls "revolt," and under this term she includes fights with authority in all its guises, experiments with language that reimagine the reach of narrative, the fashioning of sexual identities, and conflicts over tradition and heritage. These revolts can take many contradictory forms: sexual precociousness or a renunciation of sexual desire; passionate friendships where the distinction between self and other is blurred; isolation, self-mutilation, and the abnegation of bodily needs; risk-taking—extreme sports, drug use, dangerous driving—or "excessive agreeableness" (Joseph 2000); and the idealization of celebrities, politicians, beloved teachers, or even notorious criminals. If we interpret these examples of behavior as symptoms of Oedipal revolt, then we cannot interpret the risk-taking of youth as a taken-for-granted sign of pathology, or youth's compliance with authority as an indication of health or learning. Instead, we need to inquire into the particular meanings of risk in the context of youths' lives.

The Risks of Adolescents

Sex education is steeped in the language of risks: risk groups, risk behaviors, risk reduction, at-risk populations. Yet one peculiar characteristic of risk—troubling for sex education—is that it is almost impossible to convince people to see themselves at risk if they are invested in regarding themselves as safe and out of harm's way. It is a dynamic that Jonathan Silin (1995), in his study of AIDS education and early childhood education, calls "the passion for ignorance." Not knowing, refusing to see oneself as implicated, and remaining unaffected are all relations made to the risks of knowledge. Joseph Sandler (1987) calls this defense "the safety principle" and argues that safety, as an ego feeling, is a matter of perception. Following Freud's insistence that perception is not a passive process, but an active engagement with internal and external stimuli, Sandler suggests that we use our perceptive apparatus to convince ourselves that we are safe. Such persuasion is necessary because risk threatens from two directions: the pleasure principle insists that we seek out gratification even at the expense of ego stability, and the reality principle introduces into psychic life the enormous demands of sociality. The "safety principle" mediates between these two extremes and works to maintain an illusory tone of safety.

By considering safety an effect of perception and each individual's idiosyncratic meaning-making apparatus, Sandler also offers a different theory of risk. Safety comes second; it is a response to the unbearable risks inherent in psychic and social life. Safety is not something one does or achieves, nor is it an a priori state of being; rather, it is something one feels. Less a matter of action, safety is an act of interpretation. Thus, the chronology of risk is reversed for psychoanalysis: risk-taking is a symptom of loss. Adolescents who are involved in what we think of as risky behaviors may feel as if those behaviors keep them safe. And here again, we are confronted with the ways the meanings of sexuality are made in unconscious processes. Within the field of sex education, we may be elaborating a language to talk about the risks of sociality and sexual practices, but as Sandler reminds us, risk is an act of perception, a relation made to both the internal and external world. Therefore, sex education needs to consider the psychical functions of risk in a person's life. Sometimes the most unbearable experiences of risk and danger are psychical, and this psychical danger shapes how we see the world.

David Leavitt's short story "The Scene of Infection" (2001) is an occasion for readers to consider how perceptions of risk can be transformed by the affective imperatives of love, intimacy, and loss. Even HIV can be used in the youth's efforts to invent the self and secure love. In Leavitt's story, a young gay man falls passionately in love with an enthusiasm and abandon that is reserved for the uninitiated. The problem for Christopher is that his lover, Anthony, is HIV-positive, and this disparity is too much to bear. Their sero-discordant status plunges Christopher into despair. What if Anthony dies and leaves him alone? How can love be accompanied by such loss? Christopher's solution to this intolerable state of affairs is to convince Anthony to have unprotected anal sex with him so that he, too, might be infected. In Christopher's mind, infection becomes affection, and HIV is a romantic gift. The risk of being abandoned and unloved is mitigated against by the "risk" of unsafe sex.

To interpret this story as a moral lesson would forget that the entanglements of love, loneliness, and sex it describes are ordinary. For Christopher, the decision to practice unsafe sex cannot be separated from his need for love and his fear of being left behind. When he goes to the clinic to pick up his HIV antibody test results (he remains negative and disappointed), the safer-sex counselor offers a monotonous speech on the importance of protecting yourself. While this sex educator knows that the decision to have unsafe sex is complicated, and even though he recognizes the troubling ambivalence in Christopher's disappointed reaction, he has nothing to offer him but vague warnings and pamphlets describing proper condom use.

Leavitt's story is not a plea for a different kind of sex education; instead we are left with the discomforting idea that sex, including the unsafe kind, cannot be divorced from our desire to be wanted, our fears of being left alone, and our yearning for emotional intimacy. He suggests that if we want to understand why people have, crave, and enjoy unsafe sex, we need to inquire into the nature of love and its disappointments. Information about the risks of having sex, the most common tool of sex education, cannot access the nexus of love and loss that make "bug chasing" feel like a viable solution to the problem of loneliness and isolation. The lessons this story offers to sex education are multiple: we cannot separate sex from the psychological meanings we bestow on different acts of affection, sexuality is not coincident with our sexual practices, and the meanings of sexuality are made in the unconscious.

The Work of Survival

Paying attention to the psychical work of adolescence requires a great deal from the teacher and sex educator. In his writings on delinquency, Winnicott considers the difficulty that adults have tolerating the risk-taking of youth. He boldly asserts that healthy development requires some acting out. This refusal to see adolescents as pathologically ill informed his work with delinquents. In 1956 Winnicott (1992) wrote "The Antisocial Tendency," a lovely paper that outlines his theory of delinquency as a sign of hope. Arguing against the pathologization of adolescent experience, Winnicott sees acting out (including risk-taking) in adolescence as a reasonable response to an experience of deprivation. In a strange talk titled "DWW on DWW," Winnicott (1989b) gives this account of his theory:

> In delinquency, which doesn't mean anything definite, the secondary gains have become more important than the original cause, which is lost. But my clinical material brought me to the fact that the thing behind the antisocial tendency in any family, normal or not, is deprivation; and the result of deprivation is the doldrums, or hopelessness, or depression of some kind. . . . But as hope begins to turn up then the child reaches out, trying to reach back over the deprivation area to the lost object. (577)

On the question of deprivation and the loss that incites delinquency, Winnicott is generously vague. His intention is not to chastise families for failing to meet the needs of their children; he recognizes that deprivation is an ordinary and devastating experience. Winnicott (1986) offers this suitably general statement: "Things went well enough and then they did not go well enough" (91). For the child, this change leads to a sense of hopelessness. Hopelessness is a feeling of deadness, when the grounds of the self's possibility shatter. Winnicott links this feeling of hopelessness to compliance. Sometimes too much compliance signals a loss of hope: this is also a risk of adolescence. In cases of what Betty Joseph (2000) calls "agreeableness as an obstacle," risk-taking in adolescence can be an attempt to return to a moment of deprivation and loss in order to repair what went wrong. Taking risks, then, is a symptom of loss and an attempt to re-find what was lost. Risk can be a fragile place where hope turns up.

Risk-taking may be done in the name of hope and be an effort to reestablish the grounds of possibility for the self, but the actions of youth are not always hopeful. The paradox is that recognizing the tremendous psychical work of making a self in adolescence means seeing the spirit of hopefulness in acting out while insisting that risks that put the self or others in danger are not hopeful. Winnicott maintains that the initial deprivation that incited the acting out was the result of a failure of the facilitating environment, and that this second time around, adults must face the challenges of youth. What is most important for youth is that the environment be able to tolerate the aggressiveness of their risk-taking while still keeping open other, less dangerous possibilities for revolt. The parent or school must not meet youth's aggressiveness with vindictiveness, which may only aggravate superego anxiety. If, after a deprivation, children feel as though their own aggression is dangerous and will injure the people they love, in adolescence youths take risks to test the durability of their environment; the adult's responsibility is to acknowledge the losses that make development and to endure these tests. The failure of Oedipal revolt—which Winnicott compares with the fantasy of murder—must end with the parents' survival.

I am suggesting that it is useful to consider sexual activity during adolescence, especially the unsafe kind, along these lines. For Winnicott, risk-taking is posed as a challenge to adults. Refusing to recognize the reality of adolescent sexual behavior is, in essence, a refusal to meet that challenge. In contentious debates over sex education, the insistence on abstinence as the only moral and ethical choice for youth meets the challenge of adolescent sexuality with vindictiveness. However, between the abdication of responsibility and moral self-righteousness, there is what Winnicott (1986) calls "elbow room for the experience of concern." For instance, in the HBO documentary *Middle School Confessions* (HBO 2002), a twelve-year-old girl decides she is gay and nervously tells her mother. Her mother's response suggests some of the qualities of care necessary to respond generously to the challenges of adolescence. While driving her daughter to an LGBT youth group, she tells her daughter that she loves her and that when she is an adult she can date whomever she wants, but that right now she is twelve and so she is not going out with anyone. The response is thoughtful because the mother insists on the durability of the environment and still allows the girl her experience of revolt. For the experience of revolt to fail successfully requires the unwitting, but hopefully compassionate, participation and care of adults. Here hope can return as a possibility for the future.

Of course, sex educators do this important work all the time. They negotiate the administrative and political constraints within which they must operate and still offer youth a facilitating environment for experiences of revolt (cf. Weis and Carbonell-Medina 2000). In this chapter I have argued that the field of sex education must conceptualize the theoretical grounds of this work. If sex education is to become a work of survival, for both the adult and youth, then sex education needs to orient itself around narratives of sexuality that can take seriously youth's struggle to reconstruct their experience from "the absences, displacements, and deferrals of meaning" of their life history. The adolescent is, herself, searching for an interpretive practice that might help make sense of the upheavals of development and the tumultuousness of relationships. In the emotional world of the adolescent, where ambivalence reigns, sex education needs a theory of adolescent development that can see risk-taking not simply as a failure of the curriculum but as, in part, a symptom of Oedipal revolt that the curriculum can contain.

In her discussion of AIDS education, Britzman (1998b) notes that "the work of the ego places the ego at risk" (322). This observation of the fragility of the ego's defense mechanisms is equally true for the specific tasks of adolescence: the work of adolescent development places the adolescent at risk. The problem for educators is that youth use the curriculum to revolt and take risks. For instance, youth may reinterpret abstinence to mean anal sex; they may refuse to see what the threat of HIV infection has to do with them; they may fall in love with ideas their parents hate; they may remember the joy of saying no and use language to attack authority; they may relinquish speech and refuse to say anything at all; they may turn their lockers into shrines for movie stars, athletes, and singers; or they may use gym class as an opportunity to humiliate the weaker among them. In these examples—more and less risky—the formal and informal sex education curriculum provides students a site for acting out the unconscious conflicts of adolescent development. Following Winnicott, these revolts can be attempts to reach back over time and create new narratives of possibility for the self. But to do this work with interest means that the curriculum must survive the students' use of it. For educators to intervene in the sometimes dangerous and cruel risks that youth take in the name of development, we must open up spaces within the curriculum to have conversations about the pleasures and difficulties of growing up. This curriculum could be used, abused, and ultimately survive.

Intervening thoughtfully in the risks that youth take in the service of development means recognizing that our work with youth puts a certain version of the adult at risk. This is the risk of relationality: our understandings of sexuality, the self, love, and loss will be affected by our engagements with the pleasures and difficulties of growing up. In order for youth to shed the "at risk" label, we as adults must notice our own strategies for disengagement, not noticing and maintaining an illusory tone of safety. The alibis of a rigid developmental theory may keep us safe by banishing an unruly sexuality to the nether regions of adolescence.

Or, just as perniciously, we may refuse to notice the distinctions between adults and adolescents and therefore not allow youth the experience of their "immaturity." Our theory of adolescence— always cautious—should therefore be reconstructive and begin with Kristeva's insistence that adolescence is a psychical relation: adolescence does not go away. The struggles of adolescence are the struggles of being human, and the adult's task is to recognize youth's humanity.

∃ HISTORIES OF MISERY

It Gets Better *and the Promise of Pedagogy*

IN THE FALL OF 2010, in response to the media coverage of a rash of suicides by gay youth, sex advice columnist Dan Savage and his partner, Terry Miller, created a short video that directly addressed struggling gay youth. In the inaugural video of what became the *It Gets Better* campaign, Savage and Miller ask gay youth to remember that even if their high schools, homes, or towns are inhospitable, they should know that life gets better when you: leave high school, move out of your parents' house, go to college, make gay friends, fall in love, travel the world, and learn that you can have a family of your own. Their list, culled from their own autobiographies, is not meant to be exhaustive. It chronicles less the futures of gay youth than the reconstructed pasts of Savage and Miller. They tell youth that they, too, felt hopeless, survived bullying, had fights with their families, and lived to tell this story.

With this tale of survival, Savage and Miller launched an international campaign, asking LGBTQ and allied adults to make short videos that would support youth who are bullied by describing the adults' experiences of overcoming homophobic obstacles. The response has been phenomenal. At the time of this writing, over ten thousand videos have been uploaded, most from what the site calls "ordinary LGBTQ adults" (itgetsbetter. com). The videos strike a variety of affective tones: they are celebratory, painful, melancholic, and angry. They detail histories of misery—the emotional scars of having grown up in a homophobic world—and the joy at having made a good, adult queer life. Alongside these videos are messages from public figures and celebrities echoing the antibullying message that has become the convention of the site. President Barack Obama, other politicians, sports heroes, pop stars, and actors all have made videos condemning bullying.

The critical and scholarly reception for *It Gets Better*, however, has been mixed. Many applaud the proliferation of stories of lesbian and gay experience available to youth; the LGBTQ educators' advocacy group, GLSEN, for instance, has become a major sponsor of the project. Others have been critical of the homonormative tone in the narratives of *It Gets Better*, particularly Savage and Miller's inaugural video. This critique insists that it doesn't necessarily get better for everyone. If you can't go to college, leave home, and move to the big city—all places of promise in that video—then you may be a gay adult, but you will also still be poor, black, or otherwise marginalized. This critique takes aim at how the dream of a good gay life lies flush with white, middle-class values of consumption, achievement, and individuality (Puar 2012). Getting better means being college-educated, owning a home, and having children (through expensive adoptions, surrogate pregnancies, or reproductive technologies).

Alongside these critiques, many queer activists have dismissed the passivity of *It Gets Better,* insisting that it doesn't just get better. Instead, they argue, we have a responsibility, as adults, to *make it better* for LGBTQ youth. Through political advocacy, the living conditions of LGBTQ youth will be improved in schools, communities, churches, and public life. In this vein, *It Gets Better* has spawned a whole host of "Make It Better" campaigns, efforts that run alongside the original project, augmenting, interrupting, and commenting on how the issues of LGBTQ youth are being framed there.

In the support for and critiques of *It Gets Better*, education plays a starring role. Education, and high schools in particular, are responsible for the misery of LGBTQ youth, and education, as well, is understood as the cure for this misery. For instance, when GLSEN puts its support behind *It Gets Better*, one tacit assumption is that the pedagogical commitments of the project can ameliorate the effects of bullying in high school. Implicit in the critique that *It Gets Better* fails to represent the realities of all LGBTQ youth, or particular groups of queer youth, is a wish that if we craft a better lesson, a better intervention, or a more just curriculum, then marginalized youth could receive that message, without conflict, and use it to protect themselves from harassment. But just as these projects put their faith in an improved curriculum, this flat vision of education is mirrored in the homophobic belief—captured perniciously in policies that prohibit any talk of homosexuality in schools—that the absence of a curriculum similarly means that *no* lesson is being offered: if no one says "gay," then there is no risk of being homophobic. In each of these scenarios, curriculum cannot guarantee learning, and the circulation of representations of LGBTQ life through schools and among youth has effects that cannot be predicted by teachers', parents', or advocates' intentions.

In this chapter I have an oblique relationship to these critiques and a rather agnostic view of the merits of *It Gets Better* as an antihomophobic curriculum. While I take seriously the charge that in its substantive concerns, *It Gets Better* risks affirming only a narrow and relatively privileged group of young gay men, I also want to step back from the focus on these stories as curriculum to consider the contradictory ways that these narratives function. How, for instance, do these structures of address call young people into relation with LGBTQ adults? To what use do LGBTQ adults put the figure of gay youth in their narrative constructions of experience? And in what ways do LGBTQ youth take up, resist, and rewrite the narrative structures that *It Gets Better* offers them? With these questions, I signal my departure from understanding *It Gets Better* exclusively as a curricular event. I am less concerned with the politics of representation in the videos: under what conditions certain voices of queer life are positioned as exemplary or normative. Instead, I turn my attention to the pedagogical register—never far from the curricular, of course, but oriented by past, present, and future fantasies of learning. To ask how these narratives call, or fail to call, LGBTQ youth into relation with queer adults interrupts the wish that a generous or relevant curriculum could guarantee learning and shifts the focus to how pedagogical relationships between adults and youth are animated by the material and psychical conditions of address.

First, here I consider how storytelling projects like *It Gets Better* have emerged in a context where conversations between LGBTQ adults and LGBTQ youth, especially in schools, are almost verboten. The possibility of having open and honest discussions with adults in school about the pleasures and disappointments of being gay is barred to youth. The precariousness of such conversations places strict limits around what can and cannot be said, but just as importantly, shapes both how and what stories are told. We can read the ways bullying has assumed the mantle of LGBTQ issues in schools as, in part, an effect of these limits. Second, in these narratives, at once generic and moving, the structure of address is pedagogical. Here, the pedagogical structure of address creates the gay youth who are then the target of these narratives. But, equally, the structure of address also constructs the adult as teacher and mentor, allowing the adult to transform her experience into a narrative of becoming. Beginning with a close reading of the title—*It Gets Better*—I turn to Judith Butler's discussion of the transferential scene of address to comment on how both "you" and "I" are called into existence through this project. Third, I conclude by reading projects like *It Gets Better* as examples of what Christopher Nealon (2001) calls "foundling texts"—texts that instantiate a model of LGBTQ subjectivity based, in part, on shared exile from the institution of the family. In the strange temporality of these pedagogical narratives, we find a conflicted conversation happening across generations—orphan to orphan.

Early in his study of literature and melancholia, Jonathan Flatley (2008) poses a question about not getting better that puts some of the central concerns of *It Gets Better* into relief. He asks, "How long has my misery been in preparation?" (3) The question is bold. It insists that my misery has a history, that it comes from somewhere, but also that my misery requires something of me—a preparation—to remain miserable. It also strikes me as a rather grown-up question, one that we might ask as an adult about the condition of grownupness and all the disappointments and resignations of having a history that is subject to narrative. Having grown up, our misery has a history, and this history animates the present: old miseries creep into the nooks and crannies of everyday life, and new miseries amplify and modify old ones.

These histories of suffering saturate adult-youth relations. Our adolescent miseries can be prophetic, hinting at the difficulties of growing up; adulthood, when it brings compensations, often does so on the backs of youthful suffering. This may especially be the case in relationships between LGBTQ adults and youth, where the humiliations of gay adolescences survived combine with the erotic and aesthetic appeal of adolescent sexuality to create the peculiar attraction and alienation that mark much interaction between LGBTQ adults and youth. Youth are caught in a misery whose history they have yet to, or are only beginning to, narrate. This history is both theirs and ours. Youth, when writing the stories of their lives, must pass through adults' histories of misery. The intersection of the youths' narrative construction of their lives and the adults' use of their own and others' adolescences in making the history of their misery are, in this chapter, described as the emotional structure of pedagogy.

I follow these affective histories through *It Gets Better*, tracing moments of convergence and conflict—when adults call youth into certain stories of suffering and redemption, when youth respond to this hailing with gratitude or outrage or compliance—and I pay particular attention to moments when the narrative call—its formal, aesthetic, and psychic qualities—becomes more important than the stories offered. The stakes of this relation are both ordinary and urgent: Under what conditions can queer adults and youth talk to each other? How might youth find in queer adults a resource for their own history making? And how, too, might queer adults meet and survive the challenge that youth pose to our sense of order and tradition? Even posing these questions feels dangerous; the possibility of putting LGBTQ adults into contact with LGBTQ youth is exacerbated by punishing restrictions discouraging and sometimes prohibiting conversations between queer adults and youth, especially in schools. Put plainly, it is very difficult to find contexts in education where LGBTQ adults can talk to and offer support to LGBTQ youth.

In our current climate, when bullying marks and obscures LGBTQ issues in schools—and, by schools' own admission, queer students endure endemic harassment by the classmates—lesbian and gay adults remain unwelcome visitors. No one is inviting LGBTQ adults into schools to act as mentors to queer youth. As Janice Irvine (2000) insists, talk about sex in schools is fraught; leaning on discourses of the battered child, all talk about sex has the potential to be understood as a sexual act itself and, therefore, a violation of childhood innocence—especially talk about homosexuality. The conservative worry is that when queer adults talk with youth about their experiences, they do more than counsel or listen; they molest. "Sexual speech itself enacts an emotionally abusive kind of sex" (60–61); it is "a rape or molestation of the mind" (69). Fearing this symbolic collapse, we leave queer youth alone in schools.

The loneliness of this abandonment is felt on at least two registers. First, most LGBTQ youth do not have queer parents or family, and many have not met or talked with any LGBTQ adults. Their models of an adult gay life may be filled with the approbations or silence of their parents, a few out Hollywood actors, the cacophony of the Internet, and rumors of community outcasts. This colossal failure of socialization is adults' responsibility. Second, by criminalizing talk about sexuality, not only do schools become censors, but in an atmosphere where words are equated with actions, language itself is cast as risky. Queer youth who, like all youth, must turn their misery into history are left without narrative resources to make meaning out of experience.

The *It Gets Better* project addresses itself to both these scenes of poverty: it offers youth self-portraits of everyday queer adulthood, and it attempts to give youth a narrative structure to hold their misery, so that they can come to see their suffering as preparing them for an afterward. Typically in these videos, an adult details a youthful history of torment and loneliness and then domesticates that misery through claims to love, home ownership, vacations, and dogs. The narrative arc of these stories is straightforwardly pedagogical: As a teenager I was miserable but now, as an adult, I am better, and my redemptive experience should instruct yours. These narratives struggle with histories of misery that belong both to the humiliations of being gay and in high school and the disappointments and compensations of being grown-up. What fantasy of getting better, for instance, can the miserable gay adult hold on to? Here, I am interested in the shifting temporality of grownupness and the relationship between the grown-up histories of misery and the adolescent misery that is in preparation. Reading the narratives of *It Gets Better* with an interest in the competing histories that lurk beneath these conventional stories of development, I return again to consider how youth and adults are constituted through pedagogical relations.

Between "You" and "I"

The name of this project—*It Gets Better*—heralds both promise and trouble. The title is filled with ambiguity, lost referents, calls for judgment, and both optimism and nostalgia. What, for instance, is the "it" that gets better? School? Family? The community? Myself? This unmarked "it," which could be anything or everything—a person, feeling, environment, or relationship—*gets* something. "Get" in this case means "to obtain," although the verb "get" carries with it much confusion about the agency of the one who gets (OED). If it obtains something better, this improvement does not depend on anything "it" has done. And yet, even if "it" doesn't do anything—doesn't exercise its agency—it will nonetheless get something better.

The vagueness of "it" and the passivity of "gets" are only amplified when modified by "better." "Better" carries an implied comparison between the present and the future, or perhaps between the past and present, and makes the phrase even more ambiguous. It gets better than what? Better than now? Better than then? Better than others? Better than whatever I can imagine? The emptiness of this phrase, its capacity to mean almost anything and to be said by almost anyone in almost any situation, is its strength and limitation; this ambiguity makes it possible for conservative politicians, queer icons, "ordinary LGBTQ adults," and members of queer youth groups to promise, in all earnestness, "It gets better."

Yet the ambiguity of "it gets better" undoes the confident linearity—indeed, the promise—of *It Gets Better*. The lesbian or gay adult who says, "It gets better," reaches back over time and describes something that has already happened. Life was difficult, and over time, *it got better*. For the teen who says, "It gets better"—and certainly one aim of the project is to put that phrase, that confidence, in teens' mouths—the assertion is almost incantatory, reaching forward into the uncertain future and predicting an outcome. Leaning on the assurances of adults, the teen says, "It will get better." The strength and limit of *It Gets Better* is that it can potentially hold within it both "it got better" and "it will get better."

Certainly we can see the risk of collapsing "it got better" into "it will get better," but that is too easy: just because it got better for me doesn't mean it will get better for you, or just because I can tell a story of getting better doesn't mean you can tell that story, too.

Yet on this hinge between past experience and potential futures—what Jessica Fields (2012) calls "intimate possibilities" (14)—we can locate the pedagogical scene of address. In this scene, our past histories of learning and not learning meet the exuberance and outrage (if we are lucky) and the ennui and hopelessness of the young. One history of misery anticipates, invites, and conditions another. It is a dynamic that Eve Sedgwick (1993) argues inaugurates queer theory when she declares, "I think everyone who does gay and lesbian studies is haunted by the suicides of adolescents" (1). The ghosts that haunt are multiple: the dead gay teens, both past and present; contemporary gay teens we imagine are at risk of taking their own lives; but also our own adolescent selves who somehow escaped suicide and survived. In this haunting, contradictory feelings orbit around having to grow up and now being a grown-up; indebtedness and omnipotence, helplessness, envy and guilt, disappointment, and relief haunt our intellectual acts.

For the queer adult who meets in the figure of the lonely, suicidal gay teen an ideal screen for projection, this haunting—a feeling of being possessed by a familiar and strange history—dramatizes an intimate story of development. To what uses does the queer adult put the lonely gay teen in the name of growing up and getting better? And how do these uses affect how contemporary LGBTQ youth receive their welcome into queer communities and come to construct for themselves (but never by themselves) their own stories of getting better? These questions point to the pedagogy of *It Gets Better;* they signal the ways these narratives call LGBTQ youth into certain ways of inhabiting the world. This is one contribution of the *It Gets Better* project: the narratives have the potential to call young people into relation with a community of adults that, at its best, has the capacity to receive the newness youth represent with generosity and durability. Queer adults are pulling youth into conversation with queer cultures and their contested norms of love, relationships, and family, setting in motion a conversation whose direction and end cannot be known in advance.

In her study of how subjects come to occupy the pronoun "I," Judith Butler (2001) insists that our own story is called into being through our relations with an other. She describes this process as being caught between the necessity of being addressed and the risk of being stuck within the terms of that address:

> No one survives without being addressed, no one survives to tell his or her story without first being addressed, given some stories, brought into the discursive world of the story, and then finding one's way in language only later, only after it has been imposed, only after it has produced a web of relations in which one is caught, and in which one also thrives. (34)

This scene is contradictory. We are both called into being by "some stories" but then "caught" in the web those stories spin for us. "We cannot tell our story without first being addressed," Butler argues, but this address, in substance and structure, anticipates and conditions the stories we might tell about our own lives. These stories, this address, are our debt and burden, and in this way narrative enacts the limits of the pedagogical imagination.

The *It Gets Better* narratives wrestle with these conflicts around the mode of address; there is a temporal restlessness. The narratives address youth, often directly, as subjects of learning. Peppered throughout the stories are phrases like, "You need to know . . . ," and "You will learn. . . ." But what youth need to know or learn seems less important than the structure of the address. Youth will come to see themselves as being called into a pedagogical relationship. In "the discursive world of the story," adults recount histories of suffering and redemption, rhetorically place themselves in a didactic relation to youth, and—in that rhetorical move—pasts, presents, and futures are collapsed. So, even as the narratives make an explicit address to the figure of the lonely, gay teenager, named "you," and hold the adult apart, as a knowing subject named "I" (or perhaps "we"), the affective weight of this address threatens to dissolve the boundaries between "you" and "I," "you" and "we," past and present—a dissolution that many of the authors court, as in, "We did it, and we're just like you" (Savage and Miller 2011, 259).

Never is this "you" named. It remains ungendered, unspecified, and unlocated—without any particular referent but nevertheless inhabited by the ghosts of the dead teenagers who inspired this project. Tyler Clementi, the gay youth whose suicide has been tied to harassment by his college roommate, and the other dead gay youth are meant to receive this message, but always posthumously, always too late. And so this "you" asks LGBTQ youth to identify with Tyler Clementi and then to be saved by this message of hope before it is too late. If "you" are like Tyler Clementi or if "you," like Tyler Clementi, are contemplating suicide, then this narrative is meant to save you.

This is the purported structure of address of *It Gets Better:* my history as a gay adult who survived the horrors of high school and the psychological torment of feeling out of place shall instruct your experience. I survived, which means you can survive. But this pedagogy, haunted by our own histories of learning, contains another scene of address. As much as this "you" reaches out into the contemporary world of lonely LGBTQ youth, the "you" also reaches back: the other "you" to whom these narratives are addressed is the "you" that is me, albeit in another, earlier age. In this scene, the insistence that "you" will get better or stronger becomes less a prediction or promise than a historical reconstruction of experience. The third-person distance of "it gets better" is a grammatical alibi that conceals a more personal sentence: I am suffering. This is an example of the transference; past conflicts are reenacted in present situations. For Butler (2001), the narrative moves conceal "a desire whose aims are not fully transparent to me":

> So "I" tell a story to "you," and we might consider the details of the story that I tell. But if I tell them to you in the context of a transference, I am doing something with this telling, and this telling is doing something with me; it is riding a desire whose aims are not fully transparent to me. (32)

Both "you" and "I" are made up through this telling. Not only does the story offer "you" the narrative resources that will produce and limit how you tell your story, "I" also am made up through this telling, though in ways that I cannot know. In the transferential circus of *It Gets Better*, the structure of address—the positing of an "I" who speaks to a "you"—defends against a history of injury. As Butler argues, transference repeats a scene of address but in belated time, creating out of experience the life story and its undoing:

> The transference . . . operates not only in the service of narrating a life, assisting in the building of a life story, but as a force that interrupts the suspect coherence that narrative forms sometimes construct, and that can displace from consideration the rhetorical features of the scene of address, those that simultaneously draw me back to the scene of not knowing, of being overwhelmed, but that also, in the present, sustain me. (34)

In the narratives of *It Gets Better*, the "you" that structures the scene of address is necessary to the construction of my life history—a coming-out story—but that "you," split off from me and projected onto the figure of the lonely gay teen, also estranges me from myself and, following Butler, disrupts the coherence of the narrative. Our stories are always on the verge of merging and breaking apart, exposing the fundamental indebtedness and antagonism we have to the other.

Listening to or reading the *It Gets Better* stories evokes these contradictions. The narratives feel urgent and impassioned, they can deeply touch the listener or reader. At the same time, the ubiquitous turn to "you," which often comes at the end of some tortured story of harassment or near death, feels jarring—not just maudlin, but also fracturing. I find myself worrying about the lonely gay teens who might be saved by the care and concern *It Gets Better* expresses, frustrated by the clichés that fill most of the stories and also, simultaneously, addressed myself. My sixteen-year-old self needs those stories, feels affirmed, and longs for the good gay life that seemed impossible then and even now, despite my living some version of it. This is the affective logic of *It Gets Better*. We, the "ordinary LGBTQ adults" who offer our stories, suffer ourselves from this poverty. We are talking to ourselves: "I wish I knew then what I know now, but I'm happy to be able to share it with you" (Savage and Miller 2011, 207).

There is, of course, something deeply impersonal about this misrecognition, but the reach across generations, so often barred to LGBTQ youth and adults, is also poignant. While *It Gets Better* may promise to help gay youth find hope in a homophobic world, it also helps queer adults turn their experience of being miserable into history. Having made that history—sometimes for the first time—queer adults offer these stories back to youth with hope that their history will matter. Here, for instance, is Ivan Coyote's story. "It is too late for me," Coyote writes.

> I wish I had met someone queer when I was sixteen. Someone who was not ashamed of who they were, someone who I could talk to. It probably would have made my life a lot easier. I would have figured myself out earlier, and loved myself better sooner. *It is too late for me to speak to my own sixteen-year-old self*, so instead I want all of the misfits and weirdos and artists and queer kids to know a couple of things I wish someone had told me back then. It does get better. It does. (Savage and Miller 2011, 88 [emphasis added])

Coyote's text moves gracefully. The historical narrative, inaugurated in this instance with a wish, describes their own development from a sixteen-year-old someone who couldn't be figured out, who was unloved, to the adult who "knows a couple of things," most important, "It does get better." Youth inherit this concern and experience it both as care and a burden.

Consider this example. Late in the summer of 2011, a thirteen-year-old boy, Jonah Mowry, created a video expressing his trepidation about entering eighth grade since all his friends had left for high school. Sitting in front of the camera on his computer, a saccharine pop song playing in the background, Jonah silently holds up cue cards that tell his story, often looking away from the camera tearfully. Jonah describes being bullied since the first grade, thinking about suicide, cutting himself and having scars, being called "fag," and being scared about starting school in the fall. This nascent history of misery ends with a reply to *It Gets Better*: "I'm not Going any-where . . . Because I'm STRONGER Than that. And I have a *million* reasons to be Here."

Caught in what Tom Waidzunas (2012) calls "the looping effects" of discourses of gay suicide, where the ubiquity of stories of gay misery creates subjects who are miserable, Jonah constructs his story to correspond with broader social scripts about the relationship between a gay identity and suicide ideation. But his testimony also refutes his construction as a lonely, suicidal gay teen, and is addressed, in part, to the *It Gets Better* campaign. He insists that he is terribly miserable but that his unhappiness does not make suicide inevitable. It is not his gayness that makes him unhappy but rather his exile from the social worlds of the school. His video records his trepidation at returning to school with no friends.

Telling his story forward, not only does Jonah receive and rewrite the link between gayness, bullying, mental health, and loneliness, the generic structure of his narrative is borrowed. Caught in the temporal transition between "it will get better" and "it got better," Jonah turns to a representational strategy that can be traced back to Bob Dylan. Cue cards were first used in a video by Bob Dylan in 1965 in a promotion for his song "Subterranean Homesick Blues"—though every generation since has borrowed and reworked that strategy. The inheritance is apt: in that first song and video, Dylan silently holds up cards with phrases from his song playing in the background. The cards, handwritten, echo the lyrics and play with them through homonymic misspellings. The Dylan song and video, like Jonah's video, is a response to the harsh social conditions he has inherited from his parents' world. In order for Jonah to register his complaint against a culture of intolerance and indifference, he borrows his parents' language of protest. The culture he condemns also supplies him with the resources for his condemnation, which is part of the transferential structure of address that Butler insists is at the heart of subject formation and I am arguing is the emotional structure of pedagogy. We are all called into being by an address that precedes and shapes us, offering us narrative resources but also limiting what can be said. And for the LGBTQ youth who suffer from a lack of narrative possibilities as well as from physical harassment, the compromised promise of *It Gets Better* is that shared histories of misery might be the tendon of intergenerational conversation.

This promise resonates with Christopher Nealon's (2001) discussion of foundling texts. Nealon turns to mid-twentieth-century texts—the poetry of Hart Crane, Willa Cather novels, physique magazines, and the Beebo Brinker lesbian pulp novels—to trace the emergence of new narratives of lesbian and gay identity. Nealon argues that early twentieth-century lesbian and gay texts were populated by the figure of the "invert." Defined by her isolation and singularity, the invert "feels pathological." But by mid-century, a "foundling" imagination takes hold. Foundling narratives entail

> imagining, on the one hand, an exile from sanctioned experience, most often rendered as the experience of participation in family life and the life of communities and, on the other, a reunion with some "people" or sodality who redeem this exile and surpass the painful limitations of the original "home." (1–2)

Nealon describes this affective conflict as "feeling historical." Across the stories of *It Gets Better*, in Coyote's narrative, and even in Jonah's history of elementary school, we see traces of this move from exile to reunion. "Foundling" is an interesting term to describe this dynamic—defined by the OED as "a child whom there is no one to claim"; it evokes the drama of being lost and found. To be a foundling is to be an orphan, but not, according to Nealon, to be singular: foundling texts transform the isolation of the lonely, pathological invert into the promise of a community of orphans. It is, he argues, a "historiographical struggle: specifically, a struggle to find terms for historical narration that strike a balance between the unspeakability of desire, especially punishable desire, and group life" (13). It is as if for the orphan to tell the history of her life, she needs to become part of a group. This dilemma is, in essence, a reworking of Wiegman's (2012) axiom for queer theory: "It is impossible to know in advance how anyone will need to travel the distance between her desires and the world in which those desires must (try to) live" (159). For the foundling, tolerating the unspeakability of desire ironically requires finding "terms for historical narration" in the world where she must live.

This tension is played out in the *It Gets Better* narratives. There, adults try to occupy a historical narrative, charting the shift from seeing gayness as an individual pathology (through feelings of isolation, oddness, and being different, etc.) to finding oneself as part of a group, either through invocations of the family (we made our own family, chosen families, etc.) or even in participating in the video project itself. What gets better, in part, is that the lonely gay teen becomes part of a group—and certainly this is Jonah's wish and our wish for Jonah. The generosity of *It Gets Better* is that the adult, herself a foundling, addresses youth with a "you," calling them into new modes of relating.

Part of "feeling historical," which Nealon argues is so central to this new imagining of lesbian and gay identity, is coming to understand one's own history as the move from "feeling pathological" to new forms of collective life. The LGBTQ adult needs the figure of the gay youth, especially the pathological gay youth, in order to solidify this sense of having a history, rather than an affliction. *It Gets Better* stages a conversation, orphan to orphan, and calls gay youth into a community of exiles—misfits, weirdos, artists, and queer kids—where new modes of relationality can be imagined. Terry Castle, an irrepressible lesbian as well as literary historian, links the figure of the orphan to the promise of pedagogy. Bemoaning the passivity of her undergraduate students, Castle insists that leaving one's parents is necessary to remaking the world. With echoes of Winnicott and his claim that adolescents must—in fantasy—murder their parents, Castle (2011) claims that orphanhood is "a condition for world making as both the sorrow and creative quintessence of life."

This is, I think, the pedagogical ambition and limit of *It Gets Better*—that the gay or lesbian or trans- teen, orphaned, would be claimed by the queer adult, called into a shared practice of world-making; that in laying this claim, the queer adult would also, in part, be reclaiming her own lost adolescent self; and that LGBTQ youth, in being addressed, in being laid claim to, would find the narrative resources to remake our world.

4 THINKING IN SEX EDUCATION
Between Prohibition and Desire

IN THE PRECEDING THREE CHAPTERS I explored how relationships between adults and children and youth can create the conditions for a growing up that tolerates the sideways movement of development. These conditions include the compassionate care of adults, but this care always risks misrecognizing children and youth either as reflections of adults' lost histories or, if that illusion is broken, as threats to adults' sense of "grownupness." Across this study I have been asking this question: How can adults support the developmental work of children and youth when that work puts a certain version of the adult at risk? In this chapter I pull this question through another example, drawn again from debates about sex education.

An emancipatory wish stages this debate: If adults meet youth on their own terms, validate their concerns, invite them into the process of meaning-making, recognize them as complex persons, and speak in their vernaculars, can we protect youth from the conflicts and obstacles of growing up? Could such care reduce teen pregnancy, empower girls to claim their desires, guarantee healthy relationships, or smooth the process of coming out as LGBTQ? Certainly, important educational work results from this set of commitments. But these commitments, no matter how beneficent, cannot save youth from the ordinary struggle to find and create a mind of one's own. Indeed, as I have been arguing, this investment in youth can be experienced as both loving and burdensome. Youth also have the capacity to use the everyday conditions of their growing up in the service of development; punishments, approbations, and alienation that are part of the ordinary affective atmospheres of adolescence are not the royal road to bullying, poor self-esteem, and depression. Like Jonah, in the previous chapter, who is able to turn an old representational technique into a fresh condemnation of school culture, in this chapter, the prohibitions against sexual activity that youth regularly receive, ignore, and resist offer a potential space for thinking and thoughtfulness. This isn't to say that we should continue to prohibit youth from exploring their sexuality; rather, we need to recognize, as well, youth's capacity to transform the parents' no into experiments in thinking.

This inquiry centers on Julie Gustafson's documentary *Desire*, a film that follows five young women from New Orleans. The young women, in collaboration with Gustafson, discuss their hopes and aspirations while making short videos that articulate and archive aspects of their desire. I focus on Peggy, a sixteen-year-old, first-generation Chinese American student who attends a prestigious high school. At the beginning of her first short film called "The Sex Crush Project," Peggy writes lines on a classroom blackboard: "I will not talk about sex." This piece ironically captures the teenage girl's dilemma: Peggy understands her sexuality to be subject to a broad prohibition. Not only should she not "have" sex, she should not talk about it. The lines on the blackboard evoke a punitive atmosphere: talking about sex brings punishment. Indeed, her sexuality should only be talked about by others; her parents and teachers, politicians, the media, and even the documentary filmmaker who facilitates the creation of Peggy's short film all stake claims on representing young women's sexuality. But Peggy makes other uses of the prohibitions to which she is subject; she finds in them a place for thinking. The lines she writes—"I will not talk about sex"—introduce her research into the sexual lives of her friends.

Peggy's film, as well as the larger documentary *Desire*, ask how questions about sexuality might create a space where students and teachers can potentially think together about the pleasures and risks of sexuality. However, in school-based sex education for youth, especially though not exclusively in North America, conversations about sexuality are often framed by the crises of teenage pregnancy, AIDS and STIs, gay suicide, and sexual assault and harassment. These risks, real and perceived, set the agenda for a sex education constituted through discourses of moral panic and a narrow conception of health and illness. In this context, thinking can feel like both a risk and a luxury. In the United States, this fear of thinking has become enshrined in the debates between abstinence-only and comprehensive sex education. Abstinence-only sex education demands that youth say no both to sexual intercourse and to a contemporary sexualized popular culture, while advocates of comprehensive sex education respond to these prohibitions by asserting the importance of a "healthy" sexuality emphasizing birth control compliance, negotiation skills, and self-esteem (Gilbert 2010). What these approaches share is an assumption that sexuality is a risk against which education mitigates (Lesko 2010).

At its most anxious, whether abstinence-only or comprehensive, sex education demands compliance. Yet thinking is something other than compliance; it is an engagement with uncertainty and doubt and, as I explore in this chapter, it is entangled in the affective histories of sexuality that inspire the capacity to think while also unsettling the wish for understanding. Thinking is moored to love, hate, loss, and disappointment—the emotional geography of our sexual lives. These questions about the entanglement of affective histories in our epistemological longings resonate through *Desire*. When filmmaker Julie Gustafson asks young women what they want—from life, from love, and for themselves and others—the girls' responses are expectable and surprising, and through the film, Gustafson, in collaboration with the young women, explores how difficult it is to know and represent desire. In this chapter, Peggy's narrative of her desire to know about sexuality suggests the qualities of an education in sexuality that could notice the reach and effects of its prohibitions and, in doing so, come to tolerate the uncertainty of thinking.[1]

These speculations on the affective atmosphere of sex education open up debates in sex education, and in education more generally, to the intimate relationship between affect and thinking by positing a subject who is ambivalent—caught between her desire to attach to the world, to knowledge, and to others, and her desire to fend off incursions from outside. The thinking subject defends herself against knowledge—nurtures her "passion for ignorance" (Silin 1995)—but then also finds and creates her sexuality in relation to expected and unexpected objects. This subject is not in charge of her meanings, even as she uses the world to elaborate and act out internal conflicts. She is split, and this conflict—both within herself and between herself and the world—constitutes the grounds of her subjectivity and her capacity to think. With this view of the subject, conflict—and sexuality as a conflict—does not ruin education; it is the grounds of learning (Pitt and Britzman 2003).

How might we understand the work of thinking in sex education if we begin from the assumption that learning is conflicted, that sexuality resists being educated even as it inspires curiosity, and that the subject of sex education is herself divided and liable to act in her worst interest? To move theories of learning in sex education beyond compliance, we have to run the risk of centering the work of thinking. Yet thinking—understood by Freud as "an experimental kind of acting" (cited in Britzman 2009, 221)—cannot be collapsed into cognitive strategies, procedures, or attitudes. Instead, thinking is the capacity to think about one's own thoughts. It is both a move out into the uncertain world of self-other relations and a return to the equally uncertain world of self-knowledge. The pleasure and loneliness of this thinking— including the pleasure and loneliness of thinking about pleasure and what pleasures us—must become the work of sex education.

However, the obstacles to thinking and thoughtfulness lie not only in restrictive social conditions, unequal relations of power, technocratic curricula, or bad pedagogy. Thinking can feel like a risk to both the self and to others, and so we also struggle against internal obstacles. Thinking is, first of all, a capacity to distinguish between internal and external reality and to symbolize our internal worlds. Our inner worlds are marked by love and hate, injury and loss, so thinking has to pass through the affective conflicts of psychical life. As Deborah Britzman (2009) explains, "Thinking . . . will never be so far away from the absence that calls it forth" (15). One name that psychoanalysis gives to this strangely present absence is *negation*. For psychoanalysis, a negation is always double and never not about that which it disavows. However, because a negation names the idea it refuses, it displays an openness that brings it close to thinking and its obstacles. A negation, too, can be a sign of hope. In its repertoire of prohibitions, sex education has its own set of negations, and they play a contradictory role in thinking, at once repressive and punishing but also potentially liberating. And Peggy, in her reply to her culture's attempt to censure her desire, turns prohibitions—you must not talk about sex—into a personal study of sexuality's reach, asking: When you aren't talking about sex, what aren't you talking about?

In what follows, I connect the prohibitions and demands for compliance in sex education to two theories of thinking in psychoanalysis: Freud's discussion of negation and Wilfred Bion's description of the mother's capacity for thoughtfulness. Both theories of thinking and thoughtfulness challenge us to reconsider the place of thinking in sex education. Can sex education be a problem of and for thinking? How might the prohibitions that circulate through sex education create the conditions for thinking and also work to shut thinking down? To make sex education a problem of thought, we must insist that what matters most in sex education is that youth and adults are able to tolerate what is most uneducable about sexuality—its beginnings in the helplessness and omnipotence of infancy, its capacity to unsettle our sense of self and other, its sheer uselessness, its saturation with meaning, and its entanglement in relations of authority. Could we, in sex education, notice how we are mired in this difficult inventory of the human condition? That is, how might the field of sex education, in its scholarly and pedagogical practices, think at and about the limits of its own thought?

Negation and the Prohibitions of Sex Education

The history of sex education in North America is a history of prohibition, and the field has, from its inception, been concerned with limiting the scope of sexuality—its ideas, movements, and practices (Moran 2000). From early texts on the dangers of masturbation, to the nineteenth and twentieth centuries' focus on eugenics, to the contemporary obsession with abstinence and health, when the adult world has met youths' curiosity about their own and others' bodies, the adult world has said "no"—or "not yet" or "not like that." And nowhere is this "no" louder and less ambiguous than in the continuing enthusiasm for abstinence in sex education in the United States, which holds that youth should abstain from sex until marriage or, at the very least, until they are in a committed, monogamous relationship. Comprehensive sex education, the political and pedagogical antonym to the support for abstinence, advocates a broader, more holistic approach to educating youth about the pleasures and dangers of sexuality. However, despite the attempt to de-center support for abstinence, in comprehensive sex education, prohibitions still saturate the curriculum.[2] For instance, comprehensive sex education programs are themselves wedded to discourses of accountability and outcomes and measure their effectiveness almost exclusively in terms of teenage pregnancy prevention, reduction of incidences of sexually transmitted infections and HIV, delay in the onset of sexual activity, and reduction in the number of sexual partners. Jessica Fields (2008) derides this lack of imagination as a failure to envision a future for youth. Instead, comprehensive sex education is a negation, "defined more by what they hope to eradicate than what they hope to promote" (162).

Yet despite the vociferous "no" that too often surrounds youth's emergence into adult sexuality, prohibitions—no matter how plainly or loudly stated—are never straightforward. According to its own terms of success, sex education of all stripes is persistently unsuccessful.[3] It does not seem that telling youth to say no to sex, or certain kinds of sex, leads with much predictability to youth's compliance. How then can we understand the function of this impotent "no" in sex education? What work do we ask this "no" to perform?

Psychoanalysis generally regards "no" with suspicion. Beginning with his paper on negation, Freud argues that "no" does not simply mark the absence of thought; quite the opposite, a negation allows something intolerable to be admitted into thought on the condition that it is refused. Thus, in psychoanalysis, "no" is linked to the origins of thinking. When sexual activity is prohibited, it continues to circulate, under the sign of negation, through discourse and social relations pointing to the affective stakes of sex education. Like Peggy, who finds room to talk about sex by repeating the injunction to not talk about sex, the "no" is a hint as to what matters—for adults and youth.

For Freud, the capacity to say no is, in some ways, a psychical achievement. Saying no is a way of acknowledging the content of repressed thoughts, but also a way of defending against the affective significance of that content. Freud (1925) begins his enigmatic essay "Negation" with what by now has become a cliché: a patient recounts a dream and insists that he is not dreaming about his mother, to which Freud confidently replies, "So it *is* your mother!" (437). The patient, by denying that the dream is about his mother, admits that in fact the dream is about his mother. He says something more significant. For Freud, in negation an idea can enter into consciousness only when the affect originally soldered to that idea is split off and remains unconscious. The idea—for example, one's mother—can be thought in the negative, but the affect attached to that idea (hate, love, envy, guilt, etc.) must remain repressed. Indeed, the emergence of the idea is, in part, a way of protecting the self from knowing the more difficult emotional reality. This splitting produces an unaffected piece of knowledge that bears no connection to its real, emotional significance; it is what Bion (1984) describes as "denuded of meaning" (63).

At the same time, Freud optimistically links negation to the "function of intellectual judgment." Negation is a way of thinking, even if those thoughts must come out as refusals, prohibitions, or denials. As Michael Parsons (1999) explains, "Negation frees thinking from repression . . . because people who say . . . 'It's not my mother' are letting themselves be aware of something they might have otherwise obliterated . . . by virtue of saying that it does not count for anything" (69–70). For Freud, the function of intellectual judgment is honed from this compromised encounter with what cannot be fully known in the self. This psychical reality bears directly on how one reads the world outside. Rather than understanding judgment as the cognitive capacity to see "reality" as it exists, Freud (1925) insists that "perception is not a purely passive process" (238) since we are always reading the external world through our internal worlds.

Freud argues that the capacity to say yes or no, or to decide whether something is true or false, begins with the baby's first distinction between good and bad. The function of intellectual judgment follows a strange grammatical and affective trajectory. Initially we distinguish between good and bad, attributing goodness to our own selves and projecting badness into the world. In a fantastical construction that reflects the fantastical logic of the baby, Freud writes, "The judgment is: 'I should like to spit this out'; and put more generally: 'I should like to take this into myself and to keep that out.' That is to say: 'it shall be inside me' or 'it shall be outside of me'" (439). Judgments of the highest intellectual order begin in this early, cannibalistic expression of love and hate: Everything good I would like to devour, and everything bad I would like to spit out into the world. This is the origin of thinking.

Yet we can see in the transformation of grammar that Freud offers us that these emotional origins are obscured through the disavowal of the grammatical first person and the emergence of a third-person appeal to the certainty of "shall." What begins with the tentative problem of desire—"I should like . . ."—becomes very quickly the impersonal command, "It shall. . . ." In this way, Freud traces how our confident assertions about how the world is organized begin very hesitantly with the baby's frantic efforts to preserve what she feels is good inside of the self and expel what is bad and threatening out into the hostile world. For the baby, this not-yet-thinking is a problem of desire: What I want comes before what I perceive.

This dilemma surfaces in sex education for youth when the "reality" of sexuality is reduced to a series of grim statistics, scientific pronouncements, and cognitive strategies for saying no (like writing, over and over again, "I will not talk about sex"). The epistemological procedures that create "the facts about sex" split off the affective world of sexuality, so the neutrality and scientism of "the facts"—having acquired status as truth—cover over and defend against the love, hate, and conflict that inaugurate and animate our sexualities. When sex education is a set of split-off facts, "denuded of meaning," then teachers, parents, students, and researchers are protected from the difficult emotional realities that inspire and imperil our sexual lives. Indeed, as Deborah Britzman (2006) argues in her discussion of pedagogical facts, "A pedagogical fact will be affected by what it tries to influence and will repeat, through variation, the very problem it attempts to think" (153). The clinging to reality that is so pervasive in sex education repeats, through negation, these uncertain and anxious beginnings of reality. While "the facts" construct what is true or false about sexuality, such a judgment is founded on the earlier distinction between what is good or bad about sexuality. The capacity to think in sex education may begin with an engagement with "reality," but thoughtfulness emerges when the affective histories of those judgments are admitted into our conversations about sexuality.

The prohibitions we offer youth and the prohibitions that youth issue themselves can do contradictory work: saying no can be repressive and punitive, shutting down the possibility for thinking, but other "no"s can have a surprisingly generous function, allowing difficult thoughts to surface—even if in a compromised form. Prohibitions might therefore hold open the space for youth and adults to experiment with their thinking. The teacher's neutrality, her refusal to retaliate or mock naïve questions, and even the adult concern that youth should pause and think before beginning a sexual relationship can each become part of the work in sex education to think through—and help youth think through—these paradoxical qualities of prohibitions.

From Thinking to Thoughtfulness

Following Freud, thinking about prohibition and the thinking that prohibitions might allow begins with understanding desire as the grounds of our intellectual judgment. For Freud, our intellectual and emotional worlds are intertwined. Wilfred Bion, well known for taking up the problem of thinking in psychoanalysis, inherits Freud's formulation and situates thinking as a function of emotionality. For Bion, thinking is not only or even primarily a cognitive process. Thinking begins in the infant's earliest experiences of care with her mother, and like Freud's description of the baby, this early relationship is characterized by the to-and-fro of projection (spitting out) and introjection (taking in), what Bion, borrowing from Melanie Klein, describes as *projective identification.*

Bion understands the baby to be terribly helpless and thus subject to anxiety, paranoia, and fantasies of omnipotence. He theorizes the qualities of care that allow this ordinary madness to develop into a thinking apparatus and a capacity to tolerate reality. For both Bion and Freud, learning to tolerate "reality," which is partly learning to tolerate one's own limits, is central to thinking. Bion (1962) locates the beginnings of this development in the mother's capacity for reverie. Reverie is the mother's ability to receive the baby's anxious projections; to think about them, digest them, and transform them; and then offer them back to the baby in a more tolerable form. It is, very simply, the mother's capacity to think about the baby's experience. The mother, in her reverie, is able to contain what is difficult for the baby. When she gives the baby back her feelings, perceptions, and sensations in a new form, the baby is able to internalize the mother who thinks, as well as the mother's capacity for thinking and thoughtfulness. This example of projective identification is the foundation for communication between mother and infant and is, for Bion, the precondition for thinking.

This theory of thinking is based on two contentions: first, "To develop a normal mind with a sense of reality an infant must learn from experience, i.e., he must use his emotional experiences with the object to try to know them" and second, "The infant needs to be loved and known by his nurturing object" (O'Shaughnessy 1998, 186). The result of these good-enough experiences of care can be, for the baby, what Bion enigmatically calls "K," a notation he uses to disrupt our ordinary equation of knowledge with knowing something. "K" is knowledge but not "facts"; it connotes a link to the world, a capacity for learning from experience and tolerating uncertainty.

The kind of thinking that Bion would designate as "K" differs sharply from the ways learning is conceptualized in an anxious sex education. "K" cannot be equated with having a piece of knowledge. It is not evidenced by a defensive compliance, but instead, as Margot Waddell (2002) describes, it is "a capacity which resides in the more complex and arduous process of 'getting to know' something, supported by being able to tolerate both the sense of infinity (that there is always more to know) and of doubt (that is, of being able not to know)" (116). In this theory, thinking is an encounter with reality in which we can be affected by the limits of knowing "reality" and be able to think about how our perception of reality is marked by a history of helplessness and dependency. What moves us from dependence and compliance to a capacity to think for ourselves is an experience of having been thought about and, in that experience, having taken into ourselves the capacity for thoughtfulness. This is the work of a thoughtful sex education: we offer youth the experience of being thought about and, in this care for them, offer them as well our capacity for thoughtfulness.

Thinking in and about Sex Education

When youth sexuality is described as a crisis or in crisis, trusting youth to think for themselves can be difficult. The stakes feel too high; the consequences too dire. The problems that sex education must solve—teen pregnancy, HIV/AIDS and other STIs, sexual assault—require immediate action. Part of the problem is with how social, historical, and political discourses frame youth sexuality, positioning adolescence as a time of crisis (cf. Carpenter 2005; Fields 2008; Elliott 2012). The pedagogical reply to this invented crisis is to remove all ambiguity and uncertainty from the curriculum, focus on offering clear and transparent messages, and turn sexuality into a discrete and knowable set of attributes, behaviors, and identities. However, a thoughtful sex education would be less organized by what to think and how to act than by developing the capacity to think for one's self. It is a structure of address that teachers and adults must model: "I am thinking about you, and in this thinking I am offering to you my own capacity for thoughtfulness." And through this conversation that asks teachers and adults to risk their own sense of expertise, to remember their own feelings of helplessness, we could come to tolerate the ways sexuality obscures clarity, surfaces through negations and other symptoms, and troubles the barely concealed wish for omnipotence that structures sex education.

A thoughtful sex education is a risky proposition, for who will know the outcome of this education? *Desire* risks this uncertainty both by raising and representing it. Both the structure and narrative content of *Desire* represent and comment on young women's stories about their desires and the desires that adults bring to and sometimes foist on young women. The filmmaker, Julie Gustafson, spent five years in New Orleans working with and supporting a group of teenage girls as they made a series of short films on the subject of desire. These short films, written and shot by the girls themselves, are nestled into the larger film and represent a carefully constructed conversation between the young women and the adult filmmaker. Gustafson thinks about these young women's lives and, through the generic conventions of short, experimental film, offers them the experience of having been thought about and a platform for them to think for themselves (Sandlos 2011). The documentary is an archive of these relationships, and the short films exhibit a debt to that relationship and a retort; these young women are not the people Gustafson might have expected or wanted them to be or become when she started the project.

I focus here on Peggy, who uses her short films and her conversations with Gustafson to wrestle with her proximity to sex. With her opening lines, "I will not talk about sex," Peggy interjects that she thinks she is the only girl in the project "who has not had sex." In this conversation Peggy announces her distance from and closeness to the subject of "sex"; she hasn't "had sex" so she is a beginner, but this beginnerness enfranchises her curiosity. From there, the film cuts to Peggy narrating her own prohibitive views on sex: "If I ever got pregnant, it would just ruin my life, it would just completely ruin my life. I mean, I would have an abortion like that." Yet despite or because she has not had sex, Peggy also has many questions about sex. She adopts the position of a sex researcher, and in her short film she interviews her female classmates about their views. She asks, "Do girls think about sex as much as guys do?" The girls' responses suggest a capacity for thinking about their thinking. One girl says, "Girls are confused about sex. Boys know they want to have it so they think about having it. But girls are thinking about thinking about having it." This distance and recursiveness—thinking about thinking about having it—is a site of pleasure for Peggy and her subjects. Peggy and her friends circle around sex, look at it from all angles, poke at it, test its mettle, wonder what it can do for them and how it might make them feel.

Later on, Peggy asks her subjects, "So, do girls want experience?" One girl asks for clarification: "Do girls want a boy that's experienced or do they want [to] have experience?" Peggy answers, "Do they want to have the experience?" The girl replies, "Yeah. Like, once I have sex with one person, I'm gonna want to do it a lot with them. . . . I want to become familiar with them and be, like, able to experiment with them so that, if I get into another relationship, I'll know what I'm doing." Another girl continues, "I was fifteen, and I found a guy that I was very attracted to, and I was also at the peak of curiosity. There was, like, no reason not to have sex." In this exchange, sex is again linked to curiosity, and a double negation—no reason not to have sex—enfranchises these young women to explore what feels good, what they like, and what sex is for: sex is something to think about, to experiment with, to practice, and to learn from.

The attitudes that the young women display about sex in this exchange seem to demonstrate the qualities of thinking that a thoughtful sex education might hope to cultivate in young people. Yet this thoughtfulness emerges from a prohibition: Peggy frames her story as a negation—"I will not talk about sex"—in part as a response to the prohibitions about sexuality that are foisted on her by her parents, the school, and the community. But rather than only shutting down the topic, the prohibitions seem to create the conditions for this thoughtful exploration of what might get spoken about when speaking about sex. Schools may make room for talk about "the facts" of sexuality, but very rarely, and usually only accidentally or informally, would the kind of talk that Peggy elicits be admitted into formal sex education. Peggy seems to make good use of her negations, even as the prohibitions she encounters in her life are painful signs of her alienation from white, straight, southern culture. Her virginity defensively chosen, her Chineseness, her parents' religious and cultural conservatism, the school's heteronormative scripts—she turns all these constraints on sexual possibility into space to exercise her liberty to think. The short film she makes, and perhaps Gustafson herself, act as a kind of container for Peggy's sometimes confused thoughts about sex.

In another scene, Peggy takes on a task more familiar to formal sex education. She goes with the filmmaker to a pharmacy to find a spermicide she has read about in a teen magazine. Curious about the other unfamiliar products on the shelf but also nervous to be seen as curious, Peggy tries to master knowledge about sex by clinging to facts: she reads all the labels to determine which is, scientifically, the best form of contraception. But in this attempt to educate herself, Peggy not only learns the most effective method of contraception but also remembers how thinking about sex—and especially thinking about sex in public—calls up feelings of excitement, confusion, and loneliness that can put the self at risk. When a middle-aged man threatens to disturb her research, Peggy becomes nervous both because she feels she is the object of another person's judgmental gaze—in this case, a customer she worries will see her checking out condoms—and because her own incomplete knowledge cannot cure her curiosity. Indeed, while Peggy goes out into the world to search for signs of sex—to the drugstore, the teen magazine, the clothing store, the school, the abortion clinic—she also notices that sexuality doesn't just come from the outside to affect or infect us. Even as she offers important critiques of how social scripts limit the sexual lives that girls can imagine for themselves, her curiosity pushes her to seek out objects through which to elaborate her sexual selves. At their best, these objects can have a containing function and return to us bits of ourselves, once intolerable, but now made available for thinking. We meet affective parts of ourselves out in the world. The split that Freud describes, when all that feels dangerous is evacuated out into the world, has softened, and Peggy is now able to meet and think about her internal world through her engagement with those evacuated objects.

The film itself enacts this structure. Significantly, Gustafson recognizes that if these young women are to narrate stories about their own worlds, she needs to provide them with many different kinds of support. They need support learning to use a video camera, framing their shots, and constructing and then editing their stories; they need an opportunity to talk with her and with each other about their struggles to construct a story and tell a version of themselves that feels affectively rich. Yet inevitably Gustafson is the one who makes the film. She includes in it the young women's own videos, produced with her assistance; her conversations with them; their interviews of her; and her documentary footage of their everyday lives and of the public events where the young women screen their short films. Gustafson receives, thinks about, and then reconstructs the young women's stories—and not just the stories they are able to tell about their lives, but also the ones that lie below the surface, interrupt what they wanted to say, and disturb Gustafson's own sense of what she wants for them. She offers herself and her film project as a site of projective identification and then gives back to the young women a digested, worked through, flawed, but thoughtful portrait of their and her own studies in sexuality and desire.

In the process, the young women also make possible a shift for Gustafson. Over the course of the film Gustafson's desires for the young women modulate and return to her a sense of her own affective history. In one scene another young woman, herself a teen mother, turns the camera on Gustafson and asks a question that leads Gustafson to reveal that as a young woman she had two abortions. The response feels like a betrayal to the teen mother, and Gustafson looks flustered and defensive. Karyn Sandlos (2011) describes how, by including this scene and its repercussions, "Gustafson allows herself to be seen losing control of the story. . . . [In] response to difficult and unexpected questions from the adolescent, she is called on to revisit her own education in sexuality." Her own education in sexuality—including this exchange—exposes the fragility of adult authority, but like Sedgwick's description of the reparative reader, Gustafson is able to tolerate the surprise of her own history. In her conversation with the young woman and in her construction of the film, she is able to think about the surprise of sexuality.

This film can offer many lessons about the risks and pleasures of thinking in sex education and models a capacity for thoughtfulness. Bion insists that the parent must receive the child's projective identifications regardless of whether they are good or bad, think about them, and then offer them back with love and concern. What is most important for Bion is not that the parent thinks for the child, or tells the child what to think, but that the child internalizes the parent's thoughtfulness. It is the capacity for thinking that must develop in the child. The film evidences Gustafson's hope for the young women, at times veering close to a rescue fantasy, as if Gustafson, as mentor, could magically erase the social and psychological struggles that the young women face. She is not herself outside of the wish for omnipotence that structures sex education. However, the structure of the film is open enough to invite the young women into the story on their own, slightly muddled terms. The film, while the product of Gustafson's thoughtfulness, is marked by the affective worlds it portrays and the ambivalence of its subject: desire—both Gustafson's and the young women's.

Even though our affective worlds are central to our experiences of sexuality, this internal reality shadows the official curriculum, emerging in slips, laughter, anonymous questions, and furtive notes passed back and forth. The sexuality of sex education is evacuated of all those experiences we carry in us as "sexuality" in its broadest sense: our early love affairs with our parents; the mother's capacity to hold the baby's anxiety; youth's fantasies about sexuality; the adult's own tentative, unknowing experiences of sexual experimentation as a youth; and the passions and disappointments of adult sexuality. Appetite, fantasy, tentativeness, doubt, passion, loss—all these things must be spit out by a sex education that insists its version of reality is the only one that counts. Yet if we follow Freud, the insistence within sex education on the facts of sexuality, compliance with external demands, and knowledge of the right answer repeats a splitting that harkens back to the infantile. The impersonal language of sex education has passed through all those grammatical transformations that obscure the history of desire and has arrived at the dull and certain construction, "It shall . . ." How do the desires that provoke sex education become disguised in curricula as prohibitions? I have been arguing that prohibitions may be an important part of the structure of a thoughtful sex education, marking limits and thus creating a space for youth, like Peggy, to think within. How then to understand the different versions of "no" that circulate through sex education? How might we tell the difference between a repressive "no" that marks a refusal to receive the anxious projections of youth and a "no" that can return to youth the adult's capacity for thoughtfulness?

It may be too much to imagine that the field of sex education could abandon its reliance on prohibitions in their various guises. It is, after all, the adult's job to say no to the child. But we might begin to think about how an insistence that students adopt our view of their reality prohibits the kinds of thinking we would otherwise hope to nurture in youth. When it comes to sex education, we don't seem to trust youth to learn from experience. Our anxious dependence on the "facts," on scientific knowledge devoid of any contact with the contexts in which youth make decisions about their sexuality, cannot help youth come to remember their sexuality as an affective experience. Yet if we are to imagine a thoughtful sex education for youth, we must, as adults, risk thinking for ourselves, recognizing how our own desires come to structure our attempts at sex education for youth, and then offering youth generous enough prohibitions so that they can make good use of both our and their own negations as they work to craft affectively rich stories about their sexualities.

5 EDUCATION AS HOSPITALITY
Toward a Reluctant Manifesto

WHAT PLACE might sexuality have in education? Where will it arrive, and in what guise? Throughout this study, when LGBTQ sexuality has emerged in the spaces of education it is often as a controversy: battles over sex education, primary students reading about lesbian mothers, and fears of gay teachers seducing their students—all these examples illustrate the ways that sexuality sits in an often antagonistic relationship to education. In these controversies, sexuality is conceptualized as standing outside of education and as an interruption to the work of teaching and learning. Thinking about sexuality in relation to education taxes the conceptual resources we have for making sense of how we learn; even as I have insisted on the disruptive nature of sexuality I have also argued that sexuality inspires curiosity and has an adhesive quality that binds us to objects of desire, including ideas. This paradox marks the limit of education.

In earlier work Deborah Britzman and I (2004) consider the dilemma of thinking about this disruptive quality of sexuality when advocating for the full inclusion of LGBTQ students, teachers, and families in education. In that work we argue that antihomophobia education has relied on consciousness-raising as the dominant mode of narrative and model of learning, but that "the very ways consciousness-raising occurs—its attempts to offer knowledge of difference, its interest in stories of subjection and overcoming—may repress the more radical qualities of narratives of social difference" (81). Encountering these radical qualities requires a strategy of representation that exceeds what we call "the time of difficulty," when worries over homophobia structure pedagogical responses. Instead, the relationship between LGBTQ issues and education must begin with the question of how learning is tied to sexuality. Efforts to either evacuate LGBTQ issues from the space of schooling or make queer sexualities palatable and "safe" for education run the risk of also pushing curiosity, an unruly but ordinary effect of sexuality, outside of schools. The dominant focus on avoiding controversy and curing homophobia forecloses the possibility of thinking about sexuality as central to the problem of inventing a self, making friends, and learning about the world. We ask what it would mean to shift this "time of difficulty" to the "time of hospitality." Hospitality is a welcome, but one that resists idealization and risks ambivalence. Can education be hospitable? That is, can education welcome, with what the OED describes as "liberality and goodwill," whatever and whoever turns up? This is a question for kindergarten as much as for graduate school, for curriculum as much as for policy. When standing at the door of education, who will be invited in and under what conditions? Could this relation of promise and obligation offer a new model for thinking about LGBTQ sexualities in education?

Toward the end of his life, Jacques Derrida wrote a series of essays on hospitality and the challenges of greeting the foreigner. His understanding of hospitality is contradictory; he insists both that we must extend an unconditional welcome to those who arrive, and that simultaneously we must create laws, norms, and practices that are hospitable even though those laws, norms, and practices will necessarily violate the principle of unconditional welcome. It is a restless formulation. Hospitality, for Derrida and in this chapter, emerges from the conflicts between an unconditional welcome and our flawed attempts to live up to that standard. If LGBTQ sexualities are often cast as foreign, arriving at the threshold of schools as an uninvited guest, then our challenge is to greet the foreignness that is sexuality while also recognizing that our thinking will be changed in ways we cannot predict by this encounter. I follow Derrida's theory of hospitality in two directions. First, I take up the time of hospitality through three examples when queerness emerges as controversy and pushes against the limits of educational thought and practice—debates about marriage equality, stories about transgender children and youth transitioning in school, and explicit representations of sexuality in a teacher education classroom. In each example I consider how a turn to hospitality might make possible an education that welcomes queerness as both strange and ordinary in its manifestations and as a quality of experience that could be made relevant for anyone. Second, I conclude the chapter and this book with a thought experiment inspired by Derrida's commitment to the impossible project of hospitality. If we must welcome the foreigner unconditionally while instituting formal and informal practices that will necessarily violate that unconditional promise, then what might an antihomophobic and antitransphobic inquiry look like in schools? In a reluctant manifesto for welcoming LGBTQ students, families, and teachers I offer five provocations that push back against the easy confidence that any program or intervention could cure schools of social hatred while also risking a call to action. My five-point manifesto—incomplete and contingent—asks all of us who work in the many spaces and relations of education to stake a claim for queerness.

Hospitality and the Uninvited Guest

In the film *Ma vie en rose*, Ludovic, an eight-year-old boy who may be a girl, makes a grand entrance to his parents' housewarming party and surprises his family and neighbors by wearing a party dress. His parents are shocked; they jokingly call him a prankster while the neighbors remain speechless. Who has arrived? How can we make sense of this strange irruption? The film documents the parents' well-meaning efforts to understand and perhaps to tame what is most strange about their child. In doing so, they must confront what is most strange about themselves in order to encounter Ludovic's experience as something more than evidence of their failure as parents. Ludovic's elaborate fantasy life requires that his parents remember their own fantasies for their child and their family. They must make sense of the estrangement between who they imagine themselves to be—as parents, as husband and wife, and as a family—and how they are perceived by an often cruel and judgmental society. In the film, the fragile coherence of the self is pushed into crisis by an encounter with another's foreignness. This dynamic is what makes for the difficulty and the necessity of hospitality: in welcoming what seems strange in the other, we encounter our own sense of foreignness.

Derrida's (2000) essay on hospitality and the status of the foreigner takes up this projective to-and-fro and demands that we resist the idealization of hospitality. He distinguishes between the laws of hospitality and the Law of hospitality. The laws of hospitality are "the conditions, the norms, the rights and the duties that are imposed on hosts and hostesses, on the men and women who give a welcome as well as the men or women who receive it" (77). The laws of hospitality govern, with liberality and goodwill, our relations with others. These laws invoke political, legislative, and juridical domains, but they also include the informal and implicit rules and guidelines that equally govern our relations with others. But in marking limits and drawing up boundaries between proper and improper conduct, these laws of hospitality—no matter how munificent—necessarily violate the Law of hospitality as unconditional welcome:

> Let us say yes to who or what turns up, before any determination, before an anticipation, before any identification, whether or not it has to do with a foreigner, an immigrant, an invited guest, or an unexpected visitor, whether or not the new arrival is the citizen of another country, a human, animal, or divine creature, a living or dead thing, male or female. (Derrida 2000, 77)

The Law of hospitality demands that we accept what is not yet intelligible; knowledge or understanding cannot be a precondition of welcome. We are to welcome the stranger before we know who or what he or she is. These two senses of hospitality are incommensurate and yet inseparable.

Derrida is careful not to see the multiple laws as only a corruption of the Law; if it is a corruption, what he suggestively calls a "pervertibility" (79), it is because the Law of universal hospitality requires the laws of hospitality in order to be effected and not remain abstract. The move from the abstract and ideal to the juridical, political, and indeed, pedagogical requires taking a risk. Our efforts to live up to the Law of hospitality require that we imagine laws of hospitality that remain inspired by the Law even as they pervert that Law. The paradox is that no one can live up to the Law; we are, as it were, all subjects under the laws.

When sexuality arrives as a foreigner, our challenge is to imagine how we could open the doors of education to this strangeness. As the uninvited guest, sexuality shows up both predictably and unexpectedly—in the student's body, the teacher's body, and the curriculum. Indeed, its foreignness may belong to its mobility; sexuality travels across bodies, disciplines, identities, and experiences. We can never be sure where it will turn up or in what form it will manifest. Derrida reminds us that we cannot simply rest with the idea of being welcoming; such an idealization of welcome fails to consider how difficult it can be to encounter what is not yet known or understood. We must, therefore, pour our resources into imagining how we might govern that welcome. In the pedagogical moment when we enact an imperfect welcome, we must also be striving for an unconditional welcome. The universal Law of hospitality—that we should say yes to whoever or whatever turns up—is perverted by the rules and conditions for speaking about and representing a love that seems to court controversy, yet one cannot take the side of either universality or practicality. For Derrida, the relation is

> both contradictory, antinomic and inseparable. They both imply and exclude each other simultaneously. They incorporate one another at the moment of excluding one another, they

are dissociated at the moment of enveloping one another, at the moment . . . when, exhibiting themselves to each other . . . they show they are both more or less hospitable, hospitable and inhospitable, hospitable inasmuch as inhospitable. (81)

This is a strange and restless relation. The insistence for education is that ethics resides in that perverted space between the laws and the Law. Are LGBTQ sexualities problems of civil rights and codes of conduct, or do they exceed these juridical and political distinctions and include the larger question of what it means to be human? And where in education can we find the conceptual resources to tolerate the aporia between rules of civil conduct and the dream of universal welcome, the tyranny of the practical and the hyperbole of an abstract utopia? These questions ask us to approach the details of including LGBTQ sexualities in education with a commitment to protecting human rights and an attention to the ways that commitment might be enacted at the level of the curriculum, adult-child relationships, school policies and procedures, as well as our own pedagogical intentions and practices. Indeed, even as we argue for the extension of human rights to LGBTQ students, families, and teachers, we must also recognize how the concept of "human rights" itself limits how we understand our responsibilities toward each other, a problem that Derrida himself charted and which has now found critical purchase in queer theory and trans-studies (Butler 2006; Spade 2011).

Marriage Equality and Public Education

"Human rights" for LGBTQ people and communities increasingly centers on large-scale legislative reform, including campaigns for marriage equality. In jurisdictions around the world, marriage equality is being brought to legislatures and the ballot box. The fight for marriage equality is a fight for the privileges and responsibilities of civil marriage as well as the legitimacy that the symbolic act of marriage bestows on a couple. Even as the political, historical, and local contexts shape the tenor of these debates, the public conversation surrounding the extension of marriage rights to LGBTQ communities is startlingly similar in vastly different jurisdictions.

In 2005 the Civil Marriages Act passed and made same-sex marriage legal in all Canadian jurisdictions. The act declares, "Marriage, for civil purposes, is the lawful union of two people, to the exclusion of all others." This rather unremarkable description of what it would mean to spend one's life with another person, of either sex, is at the center of international conversations about the equality and status of LGBTQ communities and is echoed in similar laws throughout the world. This debate poses significant challenges to education and illustrates the tension that Derrida calls "pervertibility." When the idea of hospitality is articulated in the juridical and legislative domain, an affirmation of however people choose to live in relation to one another is lost. The Canadian act recognizes the rights of LGBTQ people who wish to marry, but it cannot recognize the multiple ways that marriages are organized, nor can it recognize and legitimate the non-matrimonial relationships that LGBTQ people might imagine and create. It is both hospitable and inhospitable—"hospitable inasmuch as inhospitable" (Derrida 2000, 81).[1]

The prospect of same-sex marriage becoming legal is also an issue of hospitality for education. Indeed, in many cases, children and the figure of "the child" play important symbolic roles in the debates about marriage equality. If teachers have a fiduciary duty to protect the civil rights of their students, how might the debate around same-sex marriage enter the classroom? When teachers and students discuss the multiple possibilities for finding love and companionship in one's life, what or who might arrive? Must teachers protect students' multiple possibilities for love, and if so, what does that protection look like? Derrida insists that we must wrestle with the difficult question of how to turn our abstract commitment to hospitality into pedagogical practices that express, in albeit imperfect ways, that commitment. Notwithstanding that children can't marry and perhaps may not even be properly called hetero- or homosexual, opponents and proponents of same-sex marriage have framed this debate as essentially pedagogical. Consider this excerpt from the widely discussed and inhospitable open letter that Cardinal Ambrožič of Toronto sent to then prime minister Paul Martin during the heat of the marriage equality debate in Canada:

> The law is a teacher. Does Canadian society as a whole, and do parents in particular, understand what the law will be teaching in this instance? It will be teaching that homosexual activity and heterosexual activity are morally equivalent. Public schools will be required to provide sex education in that light. Many parents, religious and non-religious, would not agree, nor would many, if not the majority, of Canadians. Is it fair to put children in the position of having to reconcile the values and beliefs of their parents with a novel state sponsored understanding of marriage that may not be truly supported by the majority of Canadians? (2005, A19)

What does the legalization of same-sex marriage teach students? According to this letter, the legalization of same-sex marriage could teach that there are no moral distinctions to be drawn between homosexual and heterosexual persons, that public schools must respect the rights of students to imagine themselves loving anybody, and that the state has the jurisdiction to imagine "novel" ways of governing relationships, even if that novelty is opposed by the tyranny of the majority. It is an ambitious agenda, and the anxiety this letter expresses suggests the ways that debates about marriage equality have reached out to effect larger conversations about the relationship between children and parents. Same-sex marriage is difficult, in part, because it asks us to reimagine the bonds of family.

The family is centered in debates about LGBTQ issues in education. While the rhetoric of "family values" works to exclude queers from the fold of the nuclear family, activists work to guarantee ever more access to the rights and privileges of family life: not only marriage (and divorce), but also adoption rights, pension benefits, illness and bereavement leaves, spousal support, and tax benefits. These are, as Judith Butler (2002) describes, "the ambivalent gift that legitimation can become" (17). As education wades into these murky waters, an ethics of hospitality cannot foreclose the ambivalence that accompanies any experience of family life, valued or not. It is a problem for teaching and learning: how to tolerate the tensions that contested conversations provoke. Again, Derrida is instructive. In a conversation with Elizabeth Roudinesco about the ways that gays and lesbians are remaking forms of family, Derrida (2004) does not simply equate gay and straight families or argue that all lesbian and gay families are loving; instead he offers a thoughtful provocation: *"the experiment must not be forbidden"* (emphasis in original, 33). His comment carves out a space between idealization and repudiation. Families may be idealized as the site of unconditional love and acceptance (a claim many LGBTQ people are unlucky enough to disprove even while insisting that love makes a family), but it is also remarkably difficult to become a member of a family. The family works by exclusion. Marriage equality, then, can create the conditions for LGBTQ people to have an ordinary life—with all the disappointments and hopes such a life entails.

Transgender Youth and Public Education

In the next example we meet a young person struggling to make sense of living in a body. Jade began her senior year in high school as Matt, a boy, and partway through began her transition to live as a young woman. This story is remarkable not for the controversy it caused but for the relative ease with which the school made adjustments to protect Jade from harassment. In a letter to teachers and staff, the principal outlines what he sees as the school's responsibility to welcome whatever and whoever decides to show up to learn:

> [in his letter, the principal] said Matt was a wonderful and courageous student who has the right to live as he chooses at school and in the community. "Matt will be as smart and funny and nice as

before, except he will be dressing differently in order to feel more comfortable. It is our professional duty, as board employees, to support Matt to the best of our abilities." (Scrivener 2005, A7)

What surprises in this example is not simply Matt's transition to becoming Jade but the capacity of the school community to accept this transition as part of the work of becoming oneself.

There were missteps in the school's response, and the solutions the principal came up with were not perfect. Jade was given a key to the staff washroom, in part to protect her from harassment but also out of a sense that her presence in the woman's washroom would be a threat to students. On the first day of her new life, the school counselor attended classes with Jade to answer student questions. Otherwise, she continued to attend all classes. She maintained her position as student council president. She made and lost friends over the course of the year. There were no workshops, no student assembly on transphobia. "The staff wasn't asked to prepare students. The thinking was that Jade should not be seen as an exhibit and exposed to an open forum about her change. 'We have this person who is one of us,' [the principal said], 'and we are not going to have this person hurt or embarrassed'" (2005, A6). What seems most important to the school and to Jade's parents is creating a space where Jade can explore the multiple possibilities for living in her body. In other words, the school tried to protect the ordinariness of Jade's life. Students and teachers struggled to make sense of Jade's transition. Students mixed up pronouns, wondered whether Jade was gay, and sometimes felt uncomfortable. But the principal trusted the school community to be able to tolerate discomfort and also had confidence that Jade could survive the school's transition. In a statement uncannily similar to Derrida's, a football player who did not totally understand Jade's decision was able to distinguish between his discomfort and Jade's right to live free from harassment: he said, "It was kind of shocking, but you have to allow it" (A7). In a lovely example of hospitality, this student recognizes that welcome cannot depend on his comfort, understanding, or knowledge, and the pedagogical approach at this high school recognizes that the goal of an antihomophobic and antitransphobic education cannot simply be for students to adopt positive attitudes. Learning proceeds through conflict, and wading into the confusion of pronouns may ultimately be more instructive than always saying the right thing. Learning from and not simply about Jade means confronting unsettling questions about the nature of gender. Like young Ludovic, seeing Jade work at becoming a woman reminds students and teachers that gender is work, not just for those who make a transition. What is both strange and ordinary here, for both Jade and the school community, is that our sense of who we are and what we want is not coterminous with our sexed body. Hospitality also demands that we welcome what is most foreign within the self.

Sex Instruction

For Derrida, the arrival of the foreigner returns to us our own foreignness. This is, of course, what Freud calls "the uncanny"— the strangely familiar—and at stake in this return is the flash of recognition that is defended against through feelings of horror. If an engagement with queerness can stage this return and offer a new language for thinking about the horrors of recognition and the surprise of our own foreignness, then education might learn something about its own limits from an encounter with queerness. In the last example I am reminded that, in opening the doors of education to what is foreign, we are also making space for what is foreign or strange in the self. I wanted to stage this dynamic in an undergraduate class I teach on theories of adolescence for pre-service teachers. I decided to show the Mexican coming-of-age film *Y tu mamá también* because I felt that the final, much discussed scene where best friends Tenoch and Julio kiss illustrates qualities of sexuality in adolescence: that there is bravado, the performance of a hypermasculinity, and even a vulnerability that belongs to being a beginner; but there can also be a promiscuity, a fluidity, and a narcissistic willingness to fall in love with parts of oneself in another. I thought that, insofar as queerness is foreign and not soldered to identity, the film asks us to notice first of all Tenoch and Julio's confrontation with their other selves, the selves they both are and could be. By extension I imagined the film would ask us to notice what we cannot bear to know and would therefore put into relief the contours of our own ignorance. Could the film, I wondered, prompt students to recognize their own foreignness? When I included the film, I thought I was creating the conditions to welcome queerness into the classroom as a quality of experience available for anyone. The Law of hospitality, however, demands that we do not anticipate who or what will arrive. Watching the film with the students, I may have squirmed uncomfortably through the scene where the two boys masturbate side by side while lying on diving boards, but I was most distraught when Tenoch enters their sexy, older road trip companion's hotel room in a towel and Luisa, acting as a committed teacher, offers him clear instructions on how to please her. While I had seen the film before, somehow I did not anticipate the shock of this scene. Of course, horror becomes something else less horrible if you can anticipate it. This became, for me, the queer moment in the film: my own foreignness was returned to me in the horrific image of the teacher as seducer. Tenoch is a lousy student, doesn't follow instructions, and you can see the disappointment on Luisa's face when he fails to please her. It is a disapproval I often evince.

You can invite queerness into the classroom, but you cannot anticipate what will arrive, for queerness—and here I am thinking of sexuality as what is most foreign in each of us—pushes against the laws of hospitality, is a disruptive guest, breaks rules, and is rarely a good role model. The disappointment is that you cannot put queerness in the service of socially progressive goals without foreclosing the more radical qualities of sexuality—the surprise of an awkward pronoun or an unexpected interpretation. Indeed, an engagement with queerness must risk the failure of a certain dream of education—that prejudice can be educated and identifications anticipated.

In my use of *Y tu mamá también* I imagined that it was the students' learning that was at stake in the film. What I could not tolerate was the mobility of queerness and its capacity to disrupt the stable division between teacher and student: I imagined that I was the host and that I would welcome queerness into my curriculum and pedagogy. Derrida's provocation, however, asks us to navigate that fragile and ambivalent space between the dream of the perfect lesson and the inevitability of an unexpected guest. Hospitality emerges from the conflict between what we imagine and what we can do; our commitment to justice and human rights does not, and indeed cannot, lie flush with social practices. Each example demonstrates what can happen when our ideas about embracing and honoring difference meet the conceptual, political, and psychical limitations of group living. If education is a relation of hospitality, then we will affect and be affected by our encounters with others. This relation exceeds affirmation and risks ambivalence. The challenge of welcoming queerness into education begins with a tolerance for the conflicts of learning. We might approach marriage equality through the conflicts of love and learning to live in a family, we might protect Jade's human rights most robustly if we acknowledge her ordinariness and tolerate our own sense of strangeness, and we might temper our drive to educate with a willingness to endure the humiliations of surprise. In each of these cases, I see the foundation for hospitality in education.

A Reluctant Manifesto for Welcoming LGBTQ Students, Teachers, and Families

In a focus group exploring how pre-service teachers understand their preparation to talk about LGBTQ issues in schools, I asked participants to describe what they might do if they noticed two girls holding hands in a high school hallway.[2] Several participants insisted they wouldn't even notice because they are not homophobic—for them, to notice would be to condemn. Then one participant offered that he hoped he would catch the girls' eyes and smile. In his response, unassuming and kind, he suggested that not noticing, or pretending not to notice, might be interpreted as neglectful and that showing interest could be a sign of care. This is hospitality in a minor key. For those of us who feel a slight tremble of fear as we cross the threshold of the school—even now, twenty-five years after our graduations—the possibility of a friendly smile from a teacher still has the magical ability to put us at ease.

Large-scale legal reform like marriage equality, campaigns to include LGBTQ youth and families in equity policies, comprehensive bullying prevention programs—all these major efforts to overhaul educational policy and practices hinge on small gestures of welcome that are difficult to legislate. Indeed, you cannot legislate a smile without emptying the smile of its significance, and being included in an equity policy document won't feel welcoming if upon entering the school you are treated as a stranger. I end this study with a call to imagine some conceptual shifts in our thinking about LGBTQ sexualities that might approach the dream of an unconditional welcome. What conditions are necessary for LGBTQ students, families, and teachers to experience a welcome in schools? What gestures have the potential to communicate recognition and affirmation? The reluctant manifesto I offer below spans these tensions—at once an appeal to rethink the place of LGBTQ sexualities in education and a call for our right to an ordinary life.

The manifesto has a long history in LGBTQ organizing. Valerie Solanas's 1967 "SCUM Manifesto" imagined a violent end to male supremacy, the Gay Liberation Front's 1971 "Gay Manifesto" condemned all the institutions responsible for the oppression of gays and lesbians, the "Lesbian Avengers Manifesto" (1993) inherited the direct-action ethos of ACT UP, and the "Transfeminist Manifesto" critiqued the transphobia of feminism—all these bold calls for action map queer utopias where the not yet here meets the persistent presence of the past. For José Esteban Muñoz (2010), the utopia, imagined but concrete, is a place where "queerness should and could be about a desire for another way of being in the world and in time, a desire that resists the mandate to accept that which is not enough" (96). Charting a longing for a different world, manifestos are documents of this desire, archiving histories of misery and—by declaring that this world is not enough—imagining futures that will get better. The manifesto is not prophetic—the future cannot be anticipated by our longing for it—and yet this longing pushes us out into the world and fuels our demands for change. Below, then, are proposals for change.

There is no single magic bullet that will eradicate homophobia and transphobia in education. No policy, intervention, program, or person is enough.

In this era of educational accountability, we tend to fetishize our responses to anti-LGBTQ sentiments in schools. Gay–straight alliances (GSAs) become the solution to school-based harassment, or a districtwide equity policy promises to empower teachers and principals to wipe out homophobia. A school assembly, an innovative social justice curriculum, a zero-tolerance policy on name calling, a well-loved and heroic teacher, even a reluctant manifesto—all these curricular and pedagogical talismans have been invested with the power to eradicate homophobic and transphobic hatred in schools. But none of them offer any guarantees, and not only because they aren't comprehensive enough. For a program or intervention to work, queerness must be fixed in place, the scope of the problem must be delimited, and the range of possible ways sexuality might emerge in schools be anticipated. But queerness does not answer in the place where it is called, and our attempts at mastering homophobia will be frustrated by the surprise of sexuality.

The desire to have a solution to the problem of homophobia can easily become a defense against sexuality itself. Sexuality emerges as conflict in schools and in the self, and these conflicts do not ruin education; instead, as I have argued across this study, these conflicts are themselves the grounds of teaching and learning. Our responses to homophobia and transphobia, when made in the time of hospitality, require us to learn to live in and with conflict and to understand that thinking about sexuality takes us to the limits of our knowledge. No curriculum can save us from these epistemological crises.

Everything counts—policies, programs, warm gestures, well-chosen readings, impromptu discussions, formal professional development.

Even though education cannot cure homophobia and transphobia, this does not mean that nothing matters; to the contrary, everything counts. If we are serious about creating room for LGBTQ students, families, and teachers in schools, then we have to invite those topics into the formal curriculum but also welcome them when they pop up in informal and unplanned contexts. When we respond to these arrivals, our gestures and stance reveal as much as our well-crafted equity policies.

We learn about LGBTQ issues in education all the time—in the ways these topics come up and don't come up in classrooms, the staff room, and discussions among parents. Rather than focus on always saying the right thing, we need to have confidence that the conversation that surrounds the unexpected emergence of LGBTQ sexualities in schools is itself educative, even if the debate includes hurt feelings and homophobic outbursts. Even as the debates demonstrate that LGBTQ sexualities are subject to community scrutiny, the ensuing conversation also suggests that LGBTQ sexualities are something worth talking about and that the community sanctions that conversation.

More disturbing is the absence of discussion and the ignorant belief that if you don't say anything, no one risks having their feelings hurt. As Jonathan Silin (1995) argues, ignorance is a passion—an active refusal to see one's implication in systems of knowledge. When I meet pre-service teachers who report not having discussed LGBTQ issues in their entire teacher education, this silence speaks loudly to the university's, the schools', and their own failure to see LGBTQ lives as worthy of notice. The absence is saturated with meaning.

Positive experiences of learning about LGBTQ sexuality, however, are just as likely to come from peers and informal conversations than from the formal curriculum. Conversations in hallways, making a gay friend, following a debate in the local media, or listening to a student-led presentation—these experiences can have as much of an impact as a well-designed curriculum. Part of the responsibility for the teacher or the school is to hold open spaces for these unplanned experiences to emerge.

We should hear the words "lesbian," "gay," "bisexual," and "transgender" spoken out loud, in many different contexts. We need chances to practice saying "lesbian" and "gay" with each other, so that the terms don't feel like slurs.

Our response to the problem of LGBTQ bullying has risked banishing the language of lesbian, gay, bisexual, and transgender lives to the realm of insult. For instance, significant thought has gone into how to respond to the common epithet, "That's so gay," hurled casually and cruelly through school hallways. Our pedagogical responses ask students to recognize how that phrase turns "gay" into a term of derision. One teacher told me how, when he hears that phrase, he offers a vocabulary lesson—"Do you mean, 'That's so homosexual'?"—or asks students to expand their vernaculars of putdowns—"Can you find more interesting or inventive ways to describe your displeasure?" These lessons teach students, in part, that language is important and that words can injure. But we also teach students that the term "gay" is a minefield, and if they want to avoid getting in trouble they should probably just avoid saying the word altogether.

Add to this problem the likelihood that the only other time the words "lesbian," "gay," "bisexual," or "transgender" are spoken in a school context may be in reference to bullying or sexual health. I recently attended a meeting for the LGBTQ positive space committee of a large school board. The room was filled with teachers, staff, and principals, many of whom are LGBTQ themselves, and all of whom are dedicated to finding ways to address homophobia and transphobia in schools. The conversation was circumspect in that room, even among allies; everyone seemed to have learned their lesson well. Looking at my watch, I realized we had been talking for over thirty minutes and no one had said the words "lesbian," "gay," "queer," or even "LGBTQ." Instead, we talked about inclusion and diversity and respect—all important concepts but somehow alibis for abandoning the language of sexuality. One significant obstacle we face then is finding ways to enliven these words: "lesbian," "gay," "bisexual," "transgender," "queer."

LGBTQ issues need to be seen as larger than the problem of bullying. We need to talk about LGBTQ issues when we talk about families, falling in love, seeing movies, having friends, and surviving the trials of ordinary life.

LGBTQ youth are at risk of verbal, physical, and emotional harassment in schools and in their families. Indeed, sometimes it seems as though an entire research industry has been built up around the project of tying LGBTQ youth to negative health outcomes and diminished academic success. But this effort to empirically document the lives of LGBTQ youth and so to push for changes in public and school policy does not just describe the reality of LGBTQ youth's lives; it creates them. Tom Waidzunas (2012) names the "looping effects" of discourses of gay suicide and how those constructions anticipate and, in a sense, welcome youth into the category "gay."

Recently a colleague shared a story about driving her twelve-year-old daughter to school. On the way, the daughter told her mother that she really hoped she wasn't gay. Her mother considered herself open and was shocked by what she initially understood as her daughter's homophobia. She asked her daughter why she hoped she wasn't gay, and the daughter replied that she didn't want to be depressed and kill herself. The daughter had learned the lesson offered on LGBTQ youth too well. Whereas schools teach this lesson to engender sympathy for and tolerance toward LGBTQ youth, the daughter made an additional move the curriculum didn't anticipate: rather than just be kind toward those others who are gay, she registered what it would mean to receive those lessons if she were, or were to become, gay herself.

The stories we tell about LGBTQ life in and out of schools need to proliferate. The aim cannot be just to tell triumphant stories of overcoming adversity, in the vein of the *It Gets Better* campaign; nor can we lean on the dire statistics of linking LGBTQ youth to mental health issues to shock policymakers into action. Instead, the school needs to create space for a fuller range of narratives of human experience. We need to talk about LGBTQ sexualities when we talk about the affective experiences we associate with growing up—falling in love, being bored, idolizing celebrities, feeling ugly, hating your parents. All these stories need to be available for LGBTQ students, families, and teachers.[3]

This expansion requires teachers, administrators, parents, and straight students to find ways of talking about LGBTQ issues and ideas in contexts other than health and sex education. Teachers should be able to talk about having read a gay novel, being moved by debates for marriage equality, or having a transgender friend. The lessons such casual conversations offer LGBTQ and straight students alike are that LGBTQ people are part of the community's networks of belonging and that all of our lives are enriched when we allow ourselves contact with a fuller range of human experience.

Our efforts to protect and support LGBTQ youth and children in LGBTQ families need to happen in concert with improving the working and learning conditions of LGBTQ teachers.

It is disheartening that we have divorced the rights of LGBTQ teachers from all our attention to the needs of LGBTQ students and families. That is, we expect queer teachers to take up the fight, protect LGBTQ students, start GSAs, and speak out against bullying, and yet all the while their own working conditions are often terrible and homophobic. Many LGBTQ teachers are closeted, worry about harassment from other teachers, students, parents, and administrators (Biegel 2010). This neglect has a history. Jackie Blount, in her history of LGBTQ teachers (2006), positions the current emphasis on protecting and supporting LGBTQ youth as a response to the near criminalization of LGBTQ teachers. After the successful right-wing campaigns in the late 1970s and early 1980s to vilify LGBTQ teachers as a threat to children and youth—the failed Briggs initiative, a proposition on the ballot in California in 1978 that would have deemed unfit for teaching anyone who had engaged in "public homosexual activity or conduct" came to symbolize these efforts—gay advocates turned their attention away from securing the civil rights of teachers and toward the politically more palatable work of protecting vulnerable gay teens. The neglect toward LGBTQ teachers is, in part, an effect of this history.

This history continues to structure how LGBTQ teachers understand their work. Consider a panel I organized in the fall of 2011. "Teaching Out: LGBTQ Teachers Go to School" meant to bring experienced LGBTQ teachers into conversation with LGBTQ pre-service teachers who need support with understanding how to negotiate their queerness in schools. Five teachers, representing both urban and suburban school boards in and near Toronto, were asked to talk about their experiences working in schools and to offer advice to pre-service teachers as they navigate their practice teaching placements. Yet despite the job protections and civil rights these teachers enjoy, the stories they shared about their experiences in schools revealed a pervasive climate of hostility, suspicion, and fear. The range of possibilities for being a "gay teacher" were exceedingly narrow. One teacher cast himself as hero by describing how he had become a role model to LGBTQ youth in his school following a gay student's suicide attempt. Others did not think being gay or lesbian mattered at all for their teaching, and they seemed tongue-tied when trying to describe the culture of the schools. Another told a harrowing story of a bigoted colleague and how, when he reported this behavior, he discovered that his principal was unsympathetic. Transgender teachers face an even more inhospitable environment; many invitations to participate on the panel were turned down, and I was left with the impression that it would be near impossible to be out as trans and work in a school.

A pre-service teacher leaving that panel discussion would think that either she had to be a tireless champion for LGBTQ youth, martyring herself to unfriendly and hostile principals and parents, or she would have to fade into the bland cinderblock walls of the school, developing very thick skin in order to survive the mundane and routine prejudice that fills the classroom and the staff room. If one argument of this study is that narratives of LGBTQ sexualities need to multiply in schools, this is certainly also the case for LGBTQ teachers who deserve access to stories of teaching that go beyond heroism or invisibility.

These five rather modest proposals for welcoming LGBTQ students, families, and teachers into schools emerged over the course of many conversations with teachers about the challenges of addressing LGBTQ issues in their classrooms. Many of the teachers I have spoken with feel that the obstacles to having conversations about LGBTQ issues are curricular, and likewise feel that the solutions to problems like bullying of LGBTQ students are programmatic. But just as important as these material resources are theories of sexuality that can enfranchise teachers and students alike to see conflicts about queerness as opening up spaces for teaching and learning. These conceptual resources are narratives of being and becoming LGBTQ that acknowledge our "complex personhood" and recognize how our past histories of misery and pleasure come to bear on our present preoccupations, including our yearning for a better future. If sexuality is a question that refuses the consolation of answers, if queerness disrupts the fantasies of education, and if LGBTQ students, families, and teachers deserve access to a rich narrative repertoire to organize their sense of self, then how can education rise to this theoretical occasion, holding open the door of the school without dictating the terms of entry? This question demands that education become a study of its own limits, recognizing that even as sexuality has the capacity to throw our dreams of a perfect lesson into disarray, our sexualities tether us to this world and animate our relations with others. To welcome LGBTQ students, families, and teachers into schools, we need to risk this ambivalent relation.

ACKNOWLEDGMENTS

It has taken me a long time to write this book; it has been my company for many years. Over those years I gathered many reasons to be thankful, all of which left their indelible mark on this manuscript.

Pieces of this book can be traced back to my dissertation and the mentorship I received there. Many thanks especially to Deborah Britzman, who brought me into this world of reading and writing. She continues to be a model and a measure and a very fine friend. Thanks to Alice Pitt, whose support kept me afloat and tethered me to the world of educational research; it has been my pleasure to write this book first under her deanship and now with her friendship. At York University I am privileged to work alongside remarkable thinkers, colleagues, and friends who greatly influence my research and make the hallways of York and cafés and pubs of Toronto much friendlier places. Thanks especially to Lyndon Martin, Aparna Mishra-Tarc, Jen Jenson, Mario Dipaolantonio, Lisa Farley, Don Dippo, Nombuso Dlamini, Sarah Barrett, Dan Yon, Didi Khayatt, and Steve Alsop.

At York I also am lucky to be surrounded by thoughtful students. Many attended seminars where I presented early versions of this work, read pieces of this manuscript, and offered provocative comments. Thanks especially to Mary Harrison, Julia Sinclair-Palm, Shannon Snow, and Jennifer Bethune. Michelle Miller worked with me as a graduate assistant on this project, reading and editing each chapter; she has become a valuable colleague.

I have benefited from wonderful friendships, collaborations, and conversations that are the genesis of many of the ideas in this book. Special thanks to Jessica Fields, Brian Casemore, Karyn Sandlos, Mary Lou Rasmussen, Nancy Lesko, Laura Mamo, Bronwen Low, Janet Miller, Lisa Weems, Marc Husband, Kathleen Quinlivan, Jonathan Silin, Brenda Cossman, Jude Tate, Lisa Mazzei, Rebecca Raby, Peter Aggleton, Jim Kincaid, and Dorinda Welle. Special thanks to Dr. Mark Egit for offering just enough counsel.

Thank you to Cris Mayo and Peter Taubman for their careful reading of early versions of this manuscript and to Pieter Martin for his patience and confidence in this project.

Parts of this book were completed with support from the Ford Foundation and the Social Science and Humanities Research Council of Canada.

During the final months of writing, my very best friend and cousin, Dr. Kate Bride, passed away. It is hard to imagine that she won't read this book since she runs through it and me. Many thanks to my giant family—both close and afar—for support during this difficult time and over the course of my life. Kate and I would often joke that we had educated ourselves out of our family, but clearly that is not the case. My parents, brothers and sister, aunts, uncles, and cousins all offer me a family I can call home— and as I chart through this book, that is no small accomplishment. My mother, Liz, deserves special credit for clearing a path for me and then following to see where I might end up. She is an inspiration.

Many thanks to Chloë Brushwood Rose, my dear friend, neighbor, co-conspirator, and interlocutor. Our parallel lives are sending us in such interesting directions! Thank you for the gift of your friendship.

Finally, many thanks to my most important everyday companions: to Max, for his spirited companionship, kitchen dance parties, and persistent questions, and to Jessica Fields, my best reader and favorite grown-up. All these sentences are filled with our conversations. Thank you for the life your love makes possible.

NOTES

Introduction

1. See, for example, Boldt and Salvio 2006; Britzman 1998a; Gallop 1997; McWilliams 1999; Todd 1997; Walkerdine 2001.

2. It is a lesson I take from Jessica Fields's (2008) study of sex education debates in North Carolina. Fields followed controversies about abstinence-only sex education in three counties, and in her analysis she uncovers some of conceptual complicities among groups that, politically, appear diametrically opposed. For instance, she argues that when liberal parents and school administrators support a more expansive comprehensive sex education by invoking discourses of childhood innocence, they unwittingly shore up racist ideas about black women's sexuality being always already corrupted. Similarly, Fields notices that conservative parents who oppose comprehensive sex education also have a broad and generous theory of sexuality even as they insist that heterosexual, monogamous marriage is the only legitimate site for its expression. See also Lesko 2010.

3. See, for instance, Bride 2008.

4. While I likewise hope to expand queer educational research to include the vicissitudes of sexuality and of education, I am not outside of the dilemma that Mayo and Talburt and Rasmussen designate: I am caught in the bind of having to name those bodies, relations, and desires that I am interested in thinking about in schools. In this book I pay attention to the ways that sexual and gender minorities are cast in schools as repositories for sexuality itself and how the categories we use to name sexuality, however provisional and however necessary, end up describing and limiting the range of intimate possibilities available. Throughout the study, my language risks imprecision even as I try to be careful to name what I am talking about. I most often use the acronym "LGBTQ" to gather together a panoply of gender and sexual minorities. I chose this term because it closely resembles the ways that, sexual and gender minorities are being described in schools and educational research and I want to address myself to those teachers and scholars working in and thinking about schools. Yet the acronyms we might use to describe sexual and gender minorities are ever expanding, largely in an effort to reach out to those communities whose sexualities are rendered invisible by the narrowness of mainstream gay culture: two-spirited, intersex, and asexual people, for instance. A recent call for papers for an international conference featured the acronym, LGBTTIQQ2SA*, with the asterisk standing in for all

the names yet to be invented to describe nonnormative sexualities and genders. I appreciate the political longing such an acronym enacts, but I am suspicious of the wish for comprehensiveness it represents. As Wiegman (2012) insists in her study of the disciplinary formations of women's studies, we cannot expect a name change—or expanded acronym—to repair the exclusions that the name represents. Every acronym, including LGBTQ, masks antagonisms between the terms. There are times when the interests of lesbians, gays, bisexuals, and transpeople come together and other times when they fall apart. And the Q, which I understand to designate queer, somehow has the potential to undo the tidiness of the LGBT but equally runs the risk of being made palatable because of its association with LGBT.

1. Backward and Forward

1. In December 2012 a new edition of the DSM was released, which included a new shift in the ongoing history of pathologizing queer and gender-nonconforming childhoods. Gender Identity Disorder was replaced with Gender Dysphoria, a less pathological diagnosis of gender nonconformity in childhood and adolescence and the new basis for accessing medical services necessary for transitioning. But, as Julia Serrano argues, these steps forward are not uniform. The new DSM also includes a new disorder, "travestic fetishism," which pathologizes trans-women with queer desires as "heterosexual men with a fantasy problem" (Serrano, http://juliaserano.blogspot.ca/2012/12/trans-people-still-disordered-according.html).

2. At the time of this writing, gay marriage is before the U.S. Supreme Court. Central to the arguments being made there is research demonstrating that gay men and lesbians raise well-adjusted children—meaning, in part, that their children are no more likely than their peers from heterosexual families to end up gay or lesbian themselves.

3. Stockton: "The child is precisely who we are not and, in fact, never were" (2009, 5).

4. http://blog.myspace.com/index.cfmcf.m?fuseaction=blog.listAll&frie ndID=15152043&startID=286854693&StartPostdDate=2007–07–12%20 08:38:00&next=1&page=2&Mytoken=556910D8-25C5-4261-965432939BEF2DE34566548.

5. This link between LGBTQ rights and citizenship is central to discussions of "homonationalism" in queer theory. In those conversations, scholars critique the ways that law reform projects construct the normative LGBTQ citizen who is deserving of civil rights and, in the process, disavow non-state-sanctioned forms of sociality (nonmonogamy, polyamory, singlehood) (cf. Butler 2002; Cobb 2012; Cossman 2007; Riley 2002). But further, the construction of the new, modern, rights-bearing LGBTQ citizen is often propped up by shadow figures, representing anachronistic ways of being. The best-known example of this dynamic involves the ways the trumpeting of LGBTQ rights in Israel covers over the human rights abuses of Palestinians, a practice described as "pink-washing" (cf. Schulman 2012). But this pattern is not only a feature of Israeli-Palestinian politics. Judith

Butler (2008) describes how LGBTQ rights are often set up as the pinnacle of modernity, a measure of how progressive and rational we in the West are, even while Western liberal democracies have terrible records of protecting the rights of LGBTQ people, especially when those claims for rights disrupt normative forms of kinship. Moreover, the specter of support for LGBTQ rights in the West is also used to pathologize new immigrants who arrive in the West from countries associated with Islam. Butler describes a test the Dutch government gives to new immigrants from certain countries to test their capacity to adapt to Western culture. New immigrants are shown a picture of two men kissing and then asked if the picture offends them or whether they understand the picture as representing personal liberties. Butler's reply to this test is wry: "Certainly, I want to be able to kiss in public—don't get me wrong. But do I want to require that everyone watch and approve before they acquire rights of citizenship? I think not" (5).

In Canada, a controversy over the exclusion and eventual inclusion of lesbian and gay rights in the Citizenship Guide for new Canadians was similarly fraught. When the conservative minister of citizenship and immigration, Jason Kenney, deleted mention of LGBT rights from the guide, a shocked public accused him of having a hidden (or not-so-hidden) religious agenda. But the inclusion and celebration of LGBTQ rights in the guide is not innocent. Discussions around the guide framed the inclusion of LGBTQ rights in the story of Canada as an act of public pedagogy—the guide is meant to usher new Canadians, with their potentially anachronistic views of sexuality, into the modern age. With this guide, we can proclaim: Look how progressive and modern we are! But in doing so, the guide forgets the ongoing and historical conflicts around lesbian and gay rights in Canada. Ironically, Jason Kenney recognized the stakes of the debate when he replied to criticism of his decision by saying, "I do not believe that new Canadians are potential gay-bashers." We don't want to set up support for LGBTQ rights as a test for one's Canadianness or capacity to integrate into civil society, because in doing so we risk constructing the new immigrant as backward, bigoted, premodern, and in need of enlightenment. But it is also important to see rights as emerging out of conflicts and to understand conflicts as generative and not just obstacles to equality. Our responsibility in education is not just to get everyone to give the right answer on the antihomophobia test, but to create contexts in which students and teachers can think through the collisions of private and public life that the school and other public institutions set in motion.

6.   When I first drafted this chapter I wanted to argue that you could trace the history of LGBTQ rights through children's literature. Leslea Newman, author of *Heather Has Two Mommies,* and *Belinda's Bouquet,* also wrote *The Boy Who Cried Fabulous* (2007), another children's picturebook, which features a flamboyant young boy who loves fashion and dogs and strolls in the park and whose parents seem flummoxed by his enthusiasm for everything. The boy is implicitly coded gay, and at the end of the book the boy happens upon a fabulous parade in the park. Here

gay is associated not with tolerance or overcoming bigotry but with a overflowing zest for life— a zest that is a benefit not only to him but also to his slightly befuddled parents. Similarly, Johnny Valentine not only wrote *One Dad, Two Dads,* he also wrote the more unconventional *The Daddy Machine,* a funny story of children of lesbian parents who miss having a dad and so invent a machine to make one but end up producing too many dads. However, the progress narrative I was constructing didn't quite hold. *The Daddy Machine,* certainly a complicated story of children's desires, was published in the early 1990s, and more recent books like *And Tango Makes Three* offer a domesticated portrait of family life, while *King and King,* a story of two princes who marry each other, is saturated with troubling representations of race. Yet both *Tango* and *King and King* are routinely removed from school shelves for their depictions of gay families (if penguins can be said to be gay), even as they are offered as the antidote to the lack of discussion of LGBTQ families in primary school. What is missing in my desire for a progressive history of increasing tolerance for LGBTQ families and in schools' rejection and embrace of the safe stories of LGBTQ families are the more contradictory trajectories that queerness travels through schools and the more intimate spaces of teaching and learning. The picturebooks are not the only curriculum at stake. Community debates about *Tango* inevitably teach us (and children) more about the stakes of sexuality and schooling than the story of two unusual penguins.

7. Lorraine Weir makes this point about the case in her discussion of laws regulating pornography—a risky and provocative alliance. Drawing on ancient debates about the status of visual representation and its relationship to corruptibility, Weir argues that pornography laws mistake visual representation for reality and in this symbolic collapse substitute the fantasy of an "objective person" who would be harmed by the representation for the activity of artistic creation and aesthetic judgment, both of which understand meaning to be an effect of interpretation. Like schoolchildren whose heads will be passively filled with ideas should they encounter *And Tango Makes Three,* the "objective person" who is exposed to pornography will be injured by the reality that representation is said to depict.

4. Thinking in Sex Education

1. I first encountered this film in a research project with Brian Casemore and Karyn Sandlos. In that project, we screened excerpts of the film for focus groups of teachers and sex educators and asked them to talk about the emotional stakes of sex education. My thinking about the film has been greatly influenced by those focus groups and my conversations with Brian and Karyn, both of whom have written provocative papers about the film (Casemore 2010; Sandlos 2011).

2. Over the past twenty years, debates about sex education in the United States have been framed narrowly as a fight between abstinence-only policies that condemn all forms of sexual activity outside of marriage and comprehensive sex education policies that advocate abstinence while also providing youth with information about birth control, STD prevention, and "healthy relationships." While the terms

of this debate pit abstinence against comprehensiveness as competing frameworks for sex education, the two approaches share deep similarities in their theories of learning (Lesko 2010).

3. Within the comprehensive sex education community in the United States, there is great interest in showing that sex education can positively affect "risk-taking behaviors" in youth. However, even the fiercest advocates for comprehensive sex education admit only modest results. For instance, a recent meta-analysis of evaluation studies showed that comprehensive sex education could delay the onset of sexual activity by 16 percent and reduce the frequency of partners by 14 percent (CDC 2010).

5. Education as Hospitality

1. For instance, in many U.S. states without marriage equality, corporations have extended some spousal health benefits to same sex-partners. With the passage of marriage equality laws in those states, corporations may decide to rescind those benefits unless their LGBTQ employees are married.

2. This focus group was conducted as part of a collaborative research project, "Affective Beginnings: LGBTQ Issues and Teacher Education," with Mary Lou Rasmussen, Nancy Lesko, and Jessica Fields.

3. This insistence on proliferating stories of LGBTQ sexualities in schools is central to a collaborative project I am fortunate to be a part of; "Beyond Bullying: Rethinking LGBTQ Youth and Sexualities in Schools" is a joint project with Jessica Fields, Laura Mamo, and Nancy Lesko.

BIBLIOGRAPHY

Ambrožič, Cardinal. January 19, 2005. "Letter." *Globe and Mail.*

Arendt, Hannah. 2006. *Between Past and Future.* New York: Penguin Classics.

Biegel, Stuart. 2010. *The Right to Be Out: Sexual Orientation and Gender Identity in America's Public Schools.* Minneapolis: University of Minnesota Press.

Bion, Wilfred R. 1962. "The Psycho-analytic Study of Thinking." *International Journal of Psycho-Analysis* 43: 306–10.

———. 1984. *Learning from Experience.* London: Karnac.

Blount, Jackie M. 2006. *Fit to Teach: Same-Sex Desire, Gender, and School Work in the Twentieth Century.* Albany, N.Y.: SUNY Press.

Boldt, Gail, and Paula Salvio, eds. 2006. *Love's Return: Psychoanalytic Essays on Childhood, Teaching, and Learning.* New York: Routledge.

Bride, Kate. 2008. "Pedagogical Crisis . . . Again: Reflections on the Work of Learning to Teach." In *Narrating Transformative Learning in Education,* ed. Morgan Gardner and Ursula A. Kelly, 127–44. New York: Palgrave Macmillan.

Britzman, Deborah P. 1998a. *Lost Subjects, Contested Objects: Toward a Psychoanalytic Inquiry of Learning.* Albany, N.Y.: SUNY Press.

———. 1998b. "On Some Psychical Consequences of AIDS Education." In *Queer Theory in Education,* ed. William Pinar, 321–36. London: Lawrence Erlbaum.

———. 2003. *Practice Makes Practice: A Critical Study of Learning to Teach.* Albany, N.Y.: SUNY Press.

———. 2006. *Novel Education: Psychoanalytic Studies of Learning and Not Learning.* New York: Peter Lang.

———. 2009. *The Very Thought of Education: Psychoanalysis and the Impossible Professions.* Albany, N.Y.: SUNY Press.

Britzman, Deborah P., and Jen Gilbert. 2004. "What Will Have Been Said about Gayness in Teacher Education." *Teaching Education* 15(1): 81–96.

Butler, Judith. 2001. "Giving an Account of Oneself." *Diacritics* 31(4), no. 4: 22–40.

———. 2002. "Is Kinship Always Already Heterosexual?" *Differences: A Journal of Feminist Culture Studies* 13(1): 14–44.

———. 2006. "Doing Justice to Someone: Sex Reassignment and Allegories of Transsexuality." In *The Transgender Studies Reader,* ed. Susan Stryker and Stephen Whittle, 183–93. New York: Taylor & Francis.

———. 2008. "Sexual Politics, Torture, and Secular Time." *British Journal of Sociology* 59(1): 1–23.

Carpenter, Laura. 2005. *Virginity Lost: An Intimate Portrait of First Sexual Experiences*. New York: New York University Press.

Casemore, Brian. 2010. "Free Association in Sex Education: Understanding Sexuality as the Flow of Thought in Conversation and Curriculum." *Sex Education* 10(3): 309–24.

Casemore, Brian, Karyn Sandlos, and Jen Gilbert. April 13, 2011. "On Taking an Interpretive Risk in Sex Education." *Teachers College Record*. http://tcrecord.org.

Castle, Terry. February 28, 2011. "Becoming an Orphan: Estrangement and Education." Video clip. www.youtube.com, https://www.youtube.com.

CDC (Centers for Disease Countrol) 2010. Prevention of HIV/AIDS, Other STIs and Pregnancy: Comparative Risk Reduction Interventions. www.thecommunity guide.org/hiv/Reduction.html.

Cobb, Michael L. 2005. "Queer Theory and Its Children." *Criticism* 47(1), 119–30.

———. 2012. *Single: Arguments for the Uncoupled*. New York: New York University Press.

Copjec, Joan. 2010. "The Fable of the Stork and Other False Sexual Theories." *differences: A Journal of Feminist Culture Studies* 21(1): 63–73.

Cossman, Brenda. 2007. *Sexual Citizens: The Legal and Cultural Regulation of Sex and Belonging*. Stanford, Calif.: Stanford University Press.

Derrida, Jacques. 2000. *Of Hospitality*. Stanford, Calif.: Stanford University Press.

———. 2004. *For What Tomorrow: A Dialogue*. Stanford, Calif.: Stanford University Press.

Desire. 2006. Directed by Julie Gustafson. Women Making Movies. DVD.

Duggan, Lisa. 2012. *The Twilight of Equality? Neoliberalism, Cultural Politics, and the Attack on Democracy*. Boston: Beacon Press.

Edelman, Lee. 2004. *No Future: Queer Theory and the Death Drive*. Durham, N.C.: Duke University Press.

Elliott, Sinikka. 2012. *Not My Kid: What Parents Believe about the Sex Lives of Their Teenagers*. New York: New York University Press.

Erikson, Erik. 1963. *Childhood and Society*. New York: Norton.

Farley, Lisa. 2011. "Squiggle Evidence: The Child, the Canvas, and the 'Negative Labor' of History." *History and Memory* 23(2): 5–39.

Fields, Jessica. 2004. "Same-Sex Marriage, Sodomy Laws, and the Sexual Lives of Young People." *Sexuality Research and Social Policy* 1(3): 11–23.

———. 2005. "'Children Having Children': Race, Innocence, and Schooling." *Social Problems* 52 (4): 549–71.

———. 2008. *Risky Lessons: Sex Education and Social Inequality*. Piscataway, N.J.: Rutgers University Press.

———. 2012. "Sexuality Education in the United States: Shared Cultural Ideas across a Political Divide." *Sociology Compass* 6 (1): 1–14.

Fine, Michelle. 1988. "Sexuality, Schooling, and Adolescent Females: The Missing Discourse of Desire." *Harvard Educational Review* 58(1): 29–53.

Fine, Michelle, and Sara I. McClelland. 2006. "Sexuality Education and Desire: Still Missing after All These Years." *Harvard Educational Review* 76(3): 297-338.

Flatley, Jonathan. 2008. *Affective Mapping: Melancholia and the Politics of Modernism.* Cambridge, Mass.: Harvard University Press.

Foucault, Michel. 1990. *The History of Sexuality: An Introduction.* Volume 1. New York: Random House.

Freeman, Elizabeth. 2010. *Time Binds: Queer Temporalities, Queer Histories.* Durham, N.C.: Duke University Press.

Freud, Sigmund. 1923. "The Ego and the Id." In *The Standard Edition of the Complete Psychological Works of Sigmund Freud.* Volume 19. Ed. James Strachey, 3-59. London: Hogarth Press.

———. 1925. "Negation" In *The Standard Edition of the Complete Psychological Works of Sigmund Freud, 1953-1974.* Volume 19. Ed. James Strachey, 2353-3968. London: Hogarth Press and Institute for Psychoanalysis.

———. 1930. "Civilization and Its Discontents." In *The Standard Edition of the Complete Psychological Works of Sigmund Freud.* Volume 21. Ed. James Strachey, 59-145. London: Hogarth Press.

Gallop, Jane. 1997. *Feminist Accused of Sexual Harassment.* Durham, N.C.: Duke University Press.

Georgis, Dina. 2013. *The Better Story: Queer Affects from the Middle East.* Albany, N.Y.: SUNY Press.

Gilbert, Jen. 2010. "Ambivalence Only? Sex Education in the Age of Abstinence." *Sex Education* 10(3): 233-37.

Gordon, Avery. 2004. *Ghostly Matters: Haunting and the Sociological Imagination.* Minneapolis: University of Minnesota Press.

Hanson, Ellis. 2011. "The Future's Eve: Reparative Reading after Sedgwick." *South Atlantic Quarterly* 110(1):101-19.

Irvine, Janice. 2000. "Doing It with Words: Discourse and the Sex Education Culture Wars." *Critical Inquiry* 27(1): 58-76.

———. 2002. *Talk about Sex: The Battles over Sex Education in the United States.* Berkeley: University of California Press.

Joseph, Betty. 2000. "Agreeableness as an Obstacle." *International Journal of Psychoanalysis* 81(4): 641-49.

Kaplan, Louise. 1984. *Adolescence: The Farewell to Childhood.* New York: Touchstone.

Kincaid, James. 2004. "Producing Erotic Children." In *Curiouser: On the Queerness of Children,* ed. Steven Bruhm and Natasha Hurley, 3-16. Minneapolis: University of Minnesota Press.

Klein, Melanie. 1998. "The Importance of Symbol Formation in the Development of the Ego (1930)." In *Love, Guilt, and Reparation,* 219-32. New York: Vintage.

Kristeva, Julia. 1990. "The Adolescent Novel." In *Abjection, Melancholia, and Love: The Work of Julia Kristeva,.* ed. John Fletcher and Andrew Benjamin, 8-23. New York: Routledge.

————. 2000. *The Sense and Non-sense of Revolt*. New York: Columbia University Press.

Laplanche, Jean. 1992. "Notes on Afterwardness." In *Jean Laplanche: Seduction, Translation, and the Drives: A Dossier*, ed. John Fletcher and Martin Stanton, 217–24. London: Institute of Contemporary Arts.

Laplanche, Jean, and Jean-Bertrand Pontalis. 1973. *The Language of Psycho-analysis*. New York: W. W. Norton & Company.

Leavitt, David. 2001. *The Marble Quilt: Stories*. Boston: Houghton Mifflin.

Lesko, Nancy. 2001. *Act Your Age! A Cultural Construction of Adolescence*. New York: RoutledgeFalmer.

————. 2010. "Feeling Abstinent? Feeling Comprehensive? Touching the Affects of Sex Education." *Sex Education* 10(3): 281–97.

Loutzenheiser, Lisa W., and Lori B. MacIntosh. 2004. "Citizenships, Sexualities, and Education." *Theory into Practice* 43(2): 151–58.

Love, Heather. 2007. *Feeling Backward: Loss and the Politics of Queer History*. Cambridge, Mass.: Harvard University Press.

Mayo, Cris. 2004. "Certain Privilege: Rethinking White Agency." *Philosophy of Education Archive*, 308–16.

————. 2006. "Pushing the Limits of Liberalism: Queerness, Children, and the Future." *Educational Theory* 56(4): 469–87.

————. 2007. *Disputing the Subject of Sex: Sexuality and Public School Controversies*. Lanham, Md.: Rowman & Littlefield.

McWilliams, Erica. 1999. *Pedagogical Pleasures*. New York: Peter Lang.

Middle School Confessions. 2002. Directed by Ellen Goosenberg Kent. New York: HBO Home Videos. DVD.

Mitchell, Juliet. 2000. *Feminism and Psychoanalysis*. New York: Penguin.

Moran, Jeffrey. 2000. *Teaching Sex: The Shaping of Adolescence in the Twentieth Century*. Cambridge, Mass.: Harvard University Press.

Muñoz, José Esteban. 2009. "From Surface to Depth: Between Psychoanalysis and Affect." *Women and Performance: A Journal of Feminist Theory* 19(2): 123–29.

————. 2010. *Cruising Utopia: The Then and There of Queer Futurity*. Minneapolis: University of Minnesota Press.

Namaste, Viviane. 2005. *Sex Change, Social Change: Reflections on Identity, Institutions, and Imperialism*. Toronto: Women's Press.

Nealon, Christopher. 2001. *Foundlings: Lesbian and Gay Historical Emotion before Stonewall*. Durham, N.C.: Duke University Press.

Niccolini, Alyssa. 2013. "Straight Talk and Thick Desire in *Erotica Noir*: Reworking the Textures of Sex Education in and out of the Classroom." *Sex Education*. DOI:10.10 80/14681811.2012.758037.

Odets, Walt.1995. *In the Shadow of the Epidemic: Being HIV Negative in the Age of AIDS*. Durham, N.C.: Duke University Press.

O'Shaughnessy, Edna. 1998. "W. R. Bion's Thinking and New Techniques in Child Analysis." In *Melanie Klein Today: Developments in Theory and Practice*. Volume 2. *Mainly Practice*, ed. Elizabeth Bott Spillius, 191–205. London: Routledge.

Parsons, Michael. 1999. "Psychic Reality, Negation, and the Analytic Setting." In *The Dead Mother: The Work of Andre Green*, ed. Gregorio Kohon, 59–75. London: Routledge.

Patton, Cindy. 1996. *Fatal Advice: How Safe-Sex Education Went Wrong*. Durham, N.C.: Duke University Press.

Phillips, Adam. 1997. *Terrors and Experts*. Cambridge, Mass.: Harvard University Press.

———. 1998. *The Beast in the Nursery: On Curiosity and Other Appetites*. New York: Vintage.

Pillow, Wanda. 2004. *Unfit Subjects: Educational Policy and the Teen Mother*. New York: RoutledgeFalmer.

Pitt, Alice, and Deborah P. Britzman. 2003. "Speculations on Qualities of Difficult Knowledge in Teaching and Learning: An Experiment in Psychoanalytic Research." *International Journal of Qualitative Studies in Education* 16(6): 755–76.

Probyn, Elspeth. 1996. *Outside Belongings*. London: Routledge.

Prosser, Jay. 1998. *Second Skins: The Body Narratives of Transsexuality*. New York: Columbia University Press.

Puar, Jaspir. 2012. "Coda: The Cost of Getting Better: Suicide, Sensation, Switchpoints." *GLQ: Gay and Lesbian Quarterly* 18(1): 149–58.

Riley, Denise. 2002. "The Right to Be Lonely." *differences: A Journal of Feminist Cultural Studies* 13(1): 1–13.

Rose, Jacqueline. 1992. *The Case of Peter Pan: Or, the Impossibility of Children's Fiction*. Philadelphia: University of Pennsylvania Press.

Sandler, Joseph. 1987. *From Safety to Superego: Selected Papers of Joseph Sandler*. New York: Guilford Press.

Sandlos, Karyn. 2010. "On the Aesthetic Difficulties of Research on Sex Education: Toward a Methodology of Affect." *Sex Education* 10(3): 299–308.

———. 2011. "The Enigmatic Messages of Sexuality Education: Julie Gustafson's 'Desire.'" *Sexuality Research and Social Policy* 8(1): 58–66.

Savage, Dan, and Terry Miller, eds. 2011. *It Gets Better: Coming Out, Overcoming Bullying, and Creating a Life Worth Living*. New York: Dutton.

Schulman, Sarah. 2012. *Israel/Palestine and the Queer International*. Durham. N.C.: Duke University Press.

Scrivener, Leslie. June 26, 2005. "When Matt Became Jade." *Toronto Star.*

Sedgwick, Eve Kosofsky. 1990. *Epistemology of the Closet*. Berkeley: University of California Press.

———. 1993. *Tendencies*. Durham, N.C.: Duke University Press.

———. 2003. *Touching Feeling: Affect, Pedagogy, Performativity*. Durham, N.C.: Duke University Press.

———. 2004. "How to Bring Your Kids Up Gay: The War on Effeminate Boys." In *Curiouser: On the Queerness of Children*, ed. Steven Bruhm and Natasha Hurley,

139–50. Minneapolis: University of Minnesota Press.

Silin, Jonathan. 1995. *Sex, Death, and the Education of Our Children: Our Passion for Ignorance in the Age of AIDS*. New York: Teachers College Press.

———. 1999. "Teaching as a Gay Man: Pedagogical Resistance or Public Spectacle?" *GLQ: A Journal of Lesbian and Gay Studies* 5(1) 95–106.

Singer, Linda. 1993. *Erotic Welfare: Sexual Theory and Politics in the Age of Epidemic*. New York: Routledge.

Spade, Dean. 2011. *Normal Life: Administrative Violence, Critical Trans Politics, and the Limits of the Law*. Cambridge, Mass.: South End Press.

Stockton, Kathryn Bond. 2004. "Growing Sideways, or Versions of the Queer Child: The Ghost, the Homosexual, the Freudian, the Innocent, and the Interval of Animal." In *Curiouser: On the Queerness of Children*, ed. Steven Bruhm and Natasha Hurley, 277–316. Minneapolis: University of Minnesota Press.

———. 2009. *The Queer Child, or Growing Sideways in the Twentieth Century*. Durham, N.C.: Duke University Press.

Sumara, Dennis J. 1998. "Fictionalizing Acts: Reading and the Making of Identity." *Theory into Practice* 37(3): 203–10.

Talburt, Susan, and Mary Lou Rasmussen. 2010. "'After-Queer' Tendencies in Queer Research." *International Journal of Qualitative Studies in Education* 23(1): 1–14.

Todd, Sharon, ed. 1997. *Learning Desire*. New York: Routledge.

Waddell, Margot. 2002. *Inside Lives: Psychoanalysis and the Growth of the Personality*. London: Karnac.

Waidzunas, Tom. 2012. "Young, Gay, and Suicidal: Dynamic Nominalism and the Process of Defining a Social Problem with Statistics." *Science, Technology, and Human Values* 37(2): 199–225.

Walkerdine, Valerie. 2001. "Safety and Danger: Childhood, Sexuality, and Space at the End of the Millennium." In *Governing the Child in the New Millennium*, ed. Kenneth Hulqvist and Gunilla Dahlberg, 15–34. New York: RoutledgeFalmer.

Watney, Simon. 1991. "School's Out." In *Inside/Out: Lesbian Theories / Gay Theories*, ed. Diana Fuss, 387–401. New York: Routledge.

Weir, Lorraine. 2003. "'Making Up Stories': Law and Imagination in Contemporary Canada." *English Studies in Canada* 29(3–4): 25–33.

Weis, Lois, and Doris Carbonell-Medina. 2000. "Learning to Speak Out in an Abstinence-Based Sex Education Group: Gender and Race Work in an Urban Magnet School." In *Construction Sites: Excavating Race, Class and Gender among Urban Youth*, ed. Lois Weis and Michelle Fine, 26–49. New York: Teachers College Press.

Wiegman, Robyn. 2012. *Object Lessons*. Durham, N.C.: Duke University Press.

White, Renee. 1999. *Putting Risk in Perspective: Black Teenage Lives in the Era of AIDS*. New York: Rowman and Littlefield.

Winnicott, Donald W. 1984. *Deprivation and Delinquency*. London: Tavistock.

———. 1986. *Home Is Where We Start From*. New York: Norton.

———. 1989a. "Contemporary Concepts of Adolescent Development and Their Implications for Higher Education." In *Playing and Reality*, ed. Donald W. Winnicott, 138–50. New York: Routledge.

———. 1989b. "DWW on DWW." In *Psychoanalytic Explorations*, ed. Clare Winnicott, Ray Shepherd, and Madeline Davis, 569–84. Cambridge, Mass.: Harvard University Press.

———. 1992. "The Antisocial Tendency (1956)." In *Through Pediatrics to Psychoanalysis: Collected Papers*. New York: Brunner/Mazel.

INDEX

Serrano, Julia, 106n1
Silin, Jonathan, x, 30, 37, 97
Silveira, Lucas, 14–15
Singer, Linda, 29
Stockton, Kathryn Bond, 5, 13, 15, 106n3

Talburt, Susan, xv

Valentine, Johnny, 16, 107–8n6

Waddell, Margot, 73
Waidzunas, Tom, 58–59, 98–99
Watney, Simon, 25
Wiegman, Robyn, xiv, xvi, 21, 60, 105–6n4
Weir, Lorraine, 17, 108n7
Winnicott, D. W., 26, 29, 33–36, 40–42

JEN GILBERT is associate professor of education at York University, Toronto.